C000285866

WALKING
THE
STORIES & LEGENDS
OF DARTMOOR

MICHAEL BENNIE

With maps and illustrations by Jonathan Bennie

Peninsula
Press

Published by Peninsula Press Ltd
P.O. Box 31
Newton Abbot
Devon TQ12 5XH

Tel: 01803 875875

© Michael Bennie 1995

All rights reserved. No part of this publication may be
reproduced, stored in a retrieval system, or transmitted in any
form or by any means, electronic, mechanical, photocopying or
otherwise, without the prior permission of Peninsula Press Ltd.

Printed in England by
Cromwell Press, Trowbridge, Wiltshire.

ISBN 1 872640 35 4

CONTENTS

Introduction

With its rugged terrain, its bleak and windswept landscape and its sudden mists, it is hardly surprising that Dartmoor has for centuries been a place of mystery and legend, a place where it is often difficult to tell myth from history. The area abounds in stories of pixies and witches, of rogues and ghosts, and of course of Old Dewer, the Devil himself. Some are known to be true, some are known to be false, but most have elements fact and fiction - though few would swear where one ends and the other begins!

Most of the tales have particular locations, and the moor is dotted with legendary associations - Bowerman's Nose, Jay's Grave, Childe's Tomb, Hangman's Pit and Fice's Well to name but a few. It was while walking the moor and visiting some of these spots that the idea for this book occurred to me: a collection of walks which take one to places or along routes associated with well-known Dartmoor stories. The tales themselves provide a fascinating focus, the sites are often interesting places to visit in their own right, and they are often set in some of the most majestic and beautiful scenery the area has to offer.

The book contains a variety of walks, long and short, easy and more challenging, which follow the routes and visit the sites of some of these stories and legends. The criteria I have used for selection are the interest of the story, the 'walkability' of the route and the beauty and variety of the scenery through which it passes. One or two walks which might otherwise have merited inclusion have been left out because they pass through ecologically sensitive areas. Dartmoor has been described as the last great wilderness in southern England, and it is precisely its wildness and remoteness that attract walkers. But its very popularity is putting it under heavy pressure. If we are to preserve its unique landscape, then we must treat it with respect. This means leaving as little trace of our passing as possible, and avoiding those parts which even the most careful walkers are likely to damage if they visit them in large numbers.

All the walks are circular, with the exception of Walk 1. Before describing each route in detail, I tell the story associated with it, and there is information on where each walk starts, its length and the approximate time it takes. Some of them overlap, and where this is the case I indicate which other routes they link up with in case you want to combine two walks to make a longer expedition.

I have graded the routes according to difficulty: A means short and easy, relatively flat and along well-defined paths; B means rather longer, perhaps over open ground and with one or two moderately steep ascents; and C means rather more challenging - usually over 12km (7½ miles), probably with some fairly steep climbs and almost certainly involving a certain amount of rough terrain. Rough sketch maps are provided, but the best Ordnance Survey map to use is the Outdoor Leisure 1:25,000 one, No 28.

Finally, three words of warning. First, the weather on the moor is fickle - it can change with remarkable speed and with very little warning. So if you are going any distance at all, you should be prepared for all conditions, and you should let someone know your route in case they need to call out the rescue service.

Secondly, it is not a good idea for newcomers to the moor to venture out in the mist. There are few landmarks, and in poor visibility one tor looks much like another. It is therefore easy to become lost and disoriented.

And thirdly, some of the walks take you onto the military ranges, where live firing takes place from time to time. Before venturing into these areas, you should find out the times of firing. These are published in the local press, and are also available from Dartmoor Information Centres, and from local post offices and police stations. Alternatively you can telephone Plymouth 701924 or Okehampton 52939 for recorded information. On no account venture onto the ranges (marked by red and white poles and notice boards) when there are red flags flying from the nearby hills. For ease of reference, I have indicated the walks concerned in the route summaries.

Map showing the starting points of the walks

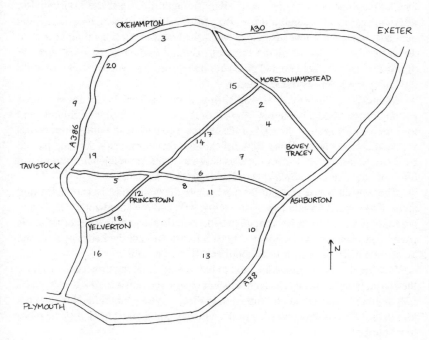

1. The Devil and Jan Reynolds

THE TAVISTOCK INN

THE STORY

Jan Reynolds was a tinner from the Widecombe area who sold his soul to the Devil. One Sunday some time later, a dark stranger rode up to the Tavistock Inn in Poundsgate and ordered a drink. He paid for it in gold, which delighted the landlady, but she became suspicious when she heard the beer sizzling as it went down his throat. Her suspicion turned to certainty when he rode off and she discovered that the gold he had given her had turned to dry leaves - it was quite obviously the Devil who had called.

Meanwhile, Jan Reynolds was sitting at the back of Widecombe church playing cards. Suddenly there was a roar of thunder and a flash of lightning, and the Devil came through the roof of the church, seized Jan and threw him across the saddle of his horse. They flew off through the stormy sky. As they passed over Birch Tor, the aces from Jan's pack of cards fell from his hand and turned into four enclosures, known as Ace Fields, as they landed.

The Warren House Inn, not far from where the walk ends, has an interesting story of its own. A traveller approached one wild and freezing winter's night and asked for a room. When he went up to bed, he noticed a chest in the corner of his room, and wondered what it was. At last his curiosity got the better of him, and he opened it. To his horror he found it contained a corpse.

Fearing that he might be the next to be murdered, he ran downstairs to raise the alarm, but was met by the landlady, who reassured him with the words, ' 'Tis only feyther.' The old man had apparently died, and they had salted him and put him in the chest until the weather broke and they could take him across the moor to be buried!

THE WALK

Start: The Tavistock Inn, Poundsgate. Grid Ref. 705721
Finish: Car park just north-west of the Warren House Inn on the B3212. Grid Ref. 675811
Parking: There is no public parking in Poundsgate. It is best to arrange to be dropped in the village if possible. If you are having a meal or a drink at the Tavistock Inn, the landlord will let you leave your car in the pub car park while you walk. If not, you can pull in off the road on the left just by the village sign at the top of the hill as you leave the village heading north. From there, walk about 200m towards the village, and where the road curves to the right, take the path to the left to join the walk. There is a small car park at the finish.
Length: 15km (9$^1/_2$ miles)
Approximate time: 4 - 4$^1/_2$ hours
Degree of difficulty: C
Links with: Walk 7
Route summary: A varied walk, combining delightful woodland scenery and open moorland with extensive views. It takes you from the place where the Devil is said to have stopped for a drink on his way to get Jan Reynolds to Widecombe itself and on to Ace Fields, where the last traces of the profligate are found. It also takes in some interesting places, including the best-known prehistoric site on the moor. Some of the walking is easy, but there are some steep climbs, especially up to Hamel Down, and some fairly rough terrain up there.

The Tavistock Inn is a beautiful, unspoilt pub. Turn left as you leave it and follow the road northwards out of the village. Where it curves sharply to the left, you will find a path leading off through a gate on the right (signposted to Lower Town and Townwood Cottages). It follows a fence along the edge of the field and at the end passes through another gate to join a drive. Once through the gate turn right and follow the lane straight down. At the bottom of a slight hill, the surfaced lane turns left. Follow it rather than taking the path straight ahead into the field. This is part of the long-distance path called the Two Moors Way, which runs across Dartmoor and Exmoor.

The lane curves left round the back of Spitchwick Manor. Follow it round (you have no alternative), but where it goes left again, take the path that leads off to the right through a gate (signposted simply 'path'). Go straight across the field and through the next gate, and then turn left to follow the hedge along the side of the next field. At the end there is another gate and another field. Continue following the hedge, pass through the next gate and go along the lane past the houses of Lower Town to join the road. Turn left.

Follow the road up the hill, looking back to admire the view over the Dart valley and South Devon almost to the sea. Pass through Leusdon, still climbing, or better still, pause for a breather outside the attractive old church on the right.

Do not take the left-hand fork at the top of the hill, but go straight on. As you do so, superb views open up to your right, across the Webburn valley. At the junction, bear right down the hill, and soon the distinctive flat shape of Yar Tor can be seen ahead.

Pass the Ponsworthy village sign, and at Forder Bridge Cross at the bottom of the hill, leave the road and go through the gate to the left (signposted to Jordan). The path runs between two hedges to another gate into a field alongside the West Webburn River. The path across the field is fairly clear, and eventually leads through another gate and into a wood. This part of the walk is delightful, along the banks of the chattering river in amongst a beautiful variety of trees.

After about 600m ($^1/_3$ mile), you cross a stile and then another, and the path leaves the river, which forms a loop to the right. They meet up again after about 100m, and you cross the river via a narrow wooden bridge. Follow the path which passes between the houses on the other side, and turn right into the lane. At the junction, go straight on up the hill.

The road passes Drywell Farm and comes out at a junction. Go straight across. The lane now passes through attractive farmland with pleasant though not spectacular views. It takes you past Dockwell Farm to another crossroads. Go straight across again and follow the road to Widecombe in the Moor. As you go, you can look back on Corndon Tor, Yar Tor and Sharp Tor. Then, as you go over the brow of the hill, a whole ridge of tors comes into view - Honeybag Tor, Chinkwell Tor, Bell Tor, Top Tor and Pil Tor - and then Widecombe village nestling in the valley, dominated by the tower which gives the church its nickname, the Cathedral of the Moor.

The road descends to a T-junction at Southcombe Cross. Turn left here (signposted Widecombe) and after a few hundred metres you will come to the village. It is an attractive place, popular with tourists because of the song 'Widecombe Fair' and therefore full of craft and gift shops and tea rooms. It is the church we have come to see, however, and the lych gate leading to it is on the right opposite the pub.

The church is worth a visit in its own right, quite apart from its associations with Jan Reynolds. It is a lovely old building, dating back to the fourteenth century, and the tower is magnificent. At the entrance, you can read a more prosaic version of what happened on that fateful Sunday in 1638. During a particularly wild storm a fireball apparently hit the tower of the church, not the Devil. Personally I prefer the legendary version.

When you leave the church, turn right outside the lych gate and pass the green on your right. After about 150m there is a lane on the left, signposted to Hamel Down for Grimspound. The lane soon becomes a track, which becomes a path between two walls and finally opens out on to moorland, climbing all the time.

Follow the wall on your right up to a finger post near the top of the ridge. At the finger post turn right along a wide and well-defined track which continues to follow the line of the wall. When the wall curves to the right, follow the track that goes with it rather than the one that goes straight ahead. When the wall turns right again to go downhill, the track leaves it and goes straight on up the hill in front. It is a steep climb, which takes you to Hameldown Beacon, from which there are superb views through almost 360 degrees.

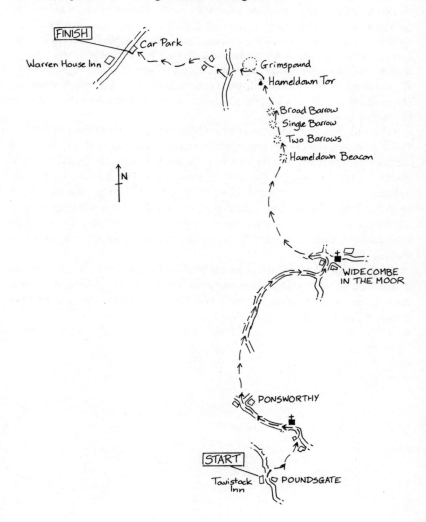

The track follows a wall on the left for a short distance, and then a line of three boundary stones on tumuli, called Two Burrows, Single Burrow and Broad Burrow respectively. These marked the boundary of the lands of Natsworthy Manor. At Broad Burrow, the track bears left past the remains of Hameldown Cross, which was used as another boundary stone (you can make out the initials DS on it, standing for Duke of Somerset, the Lord of the Manor of Natsworthy) and on to Hameldown Tor.

Pass the cairn on Hameldown Tor and follow the track down a steep hill to Grimspound, an interesting prehistoric settlement with its boundary wall still largely intact and the remains of a few huts inside. Turn left here, and take the path down to the road. Make for the wall ahead of you across the road and turn right onto the track to Headland Warren Farm. Go through the farm gate and straight on (signposted to Warren House Inn). Pass the farm on your right and go through another gate. At the finger post ahead of you, turn left (signposted to Warren House Inn again). A well-worn path follows the line of telephone poles. Notice the stone row on your left. A little further on, the summit of Birch Tor can be seen on your right.

The path goes down the hill, past a wall on the left. This is one of the Ace Fields. The path you are on crosses another track at the bottom of the valley and climbs the other side. Look back as you near the top of the climb, and you will clearly see the four Ace Fields on the opposite slope. The one on the far left is definitely diamond-shaped, and the next along has the rough form of a heart from this angle. The third, near the bottom of the valley, is an odd shape which, with a bit of imagination could be a club. However, it takes considerable imagination to make a spade of the one on the far right (the one you passed on the way down)!

At the top of the hill, you will see the Warren House Inn to your left. Fork left to reach the small car park and the end of the walk, or follow the line of the road down to the Warren House Inn for a rather better welcome than the terrified visitor of yore received!

2. The Last Journey of Kitty Jay

JAY'S GRAVE

THE STORY

Kitty Jay is said to have been a workhouse girl who worked on a farm in the Manaton area. Like many a lass before and since, she was seduced by a young man who disowned her when she became pregnant. In despair, she hanged herself.

According to the landlord of the Ring of Bells in North Bovey, she did so at that pub. Most versions of the story say simply that she hanged herself in a barn, but it could just as easily have been a barn attached to the pub as anywhere else! One thing *is* known: a previous landlady refused to sleep on the premises, claiming that the inn was haunted.

Being a suicide, Kitty could not be buried in consecrated ground. She was therefore interred at a crossroads with a stake through her heart. This was believed to stop the Devil getting her soul, and at the same time confuse her spirit so that it could not find its way back to haunt the living. If the story told at the Ring of Bells is to be believed, however, this precaution obviously did not work!

You will usually find a bunch of fresh flowers on Jay's Grave. It is said that there has never been a day when flowers have not appeared there, even in midwinter, apparently brought by the pixies.

THE WALK

Start and Finish: The Ring of Bells, North Bovey. Grid Ref. 741839
Parking: In the free car park opposite the church.
Length: 13km (8 miles)
Approximate time: 3½ - 4 hours
Degree of difficulty: B/C

Route summary: The walk takes you from the place where Kitty Jay is said in some versions of the story to have committed suicide to her grave. It is an attractive and varied route, taking in moorland, woods and farmland. It is quite long but generally undemanding. There is just one steep climb up Easdon Down, but some of the farm fields can become very muddy in wet weather. There is a fair amount of road walking, but since they are minor roads with little traffic, even that is not unpleasant.

North Bovey is a charming village, completely off the beaten track, and the Ring of Bells is a delightful old pub. From the pub, go down the left-hand side of the green, and turn left on to the road to Manaton. Pass the church on your right and follow the road down to the river and up the other side. A few hundred metres past Aller, take the bridleway leading off to the right just beyond a group of houses (signposted to Barracott via Easdon).

It is a wide track between walls, and at the end is a gate leading into a wood. Go through the gate and turn immediately to the right up a slope to meet a track. Follow this until you come to another track. Go straight across and continue to a gate which leads out of the wood and on to Easdon Down.

Once out of the wood, your way lies straight up the hill. The path is not always clear, but if you follow the stream you can pick your way through the bracken fairly easily. Alternatively, you could keep to the wall on your right. When the wall curves away to the right, you should turn half left, aiming for the far corner of the wood, which is just visible on the horizon. As you climb, pause to admire the beautiful view across the River Bovey to Lustleigh Cleave.

Skirt the corner and follow the path which now contours round Easdon Tor. As you round the corner, another magnificent panorama opens up, with Hayne Down in the foreground and the unmistakable shapes of Hound Tor and Haytor beyond.

The path takes you to the corner of a boundary wall. Follow the right-hand wall until it turns left, then follow it down the hill to meet a lane at the bottom. Go through the gate on the left and down the lane to join the B3344. Turn right. About 200m or so down this road, you will pass Canna Farm, set some way back on the right. According to some accounts, this is the farm where Kitty Jay worked. At Heatree Cross, about 1km ($^1/_2$ mile) further on, turn left (signposted to Hound Tor, Haytor and Widecombe). This is an attractive road, with a pretty woodland on the right and Cripdon Down on the left. After a little more than 1km (about $^3/_4$ mile), you will find Jay's Grave on your right. If you would rather not walk on the road, you can cut up to Cripdon Down. Keep to the general line of the road, and you will eventually come to a fence. Turn right at the fence, and the path will take you straight to the grave.

At the grave, follow the bridleway which leads off to the right between two boundary walls, signposted to Natsworthy Gate. As you go, pause along the way to admire the view over Widecombe on your left. When you come to the road, turn left and then almost immediately right through a gate. After the gate, turn right again (signposted to Moorgate). Cross a stile into a wood and take the path that leads straight on. Although there are a number of foresters' tracks, the path you want is waymarked in yellow on some of the trees. Moreover, if you keep the sound of the river (which you will only occasionally see through the trees) on your right, you will be heading the right way.

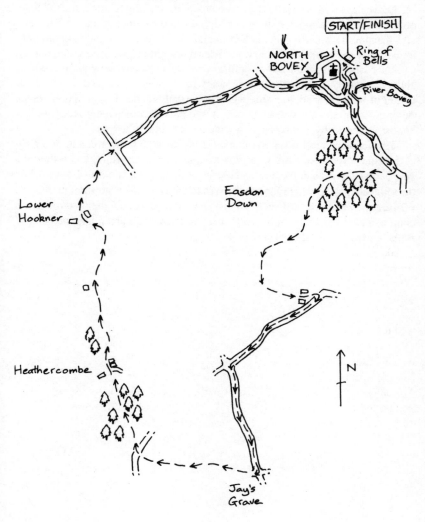

The path takes an almost straight line through the wood and brings you to what looks like open country, but is in fact just a temporary break in the trees. Cross the field in front of you, heading for a small group of houses. Pass the houses, cross a road and climb over two stiles to re-enter the wood on the other side. Bear right immediately after the second stile, and after about 100m bear left and immediately right again. (This may seem complicated, but as long as you remember to keep looking out for the yellow waymarks, it is difficult to go wrong.)

Leave the wood via a stile and cross two fields, making for the farm buildings on the far side. A large yellow square high up on the corner of one of them tells you that this is still the waymarked path. This is where it can become very muddy if it has been wet, so beware, especially around the gate at the corner. Cross the lane to another gateway (still waymarked in yellow, and equally muddy). Head diagonally right across two fields. Cross a stream, then make for the far corner of the next field, to a stile which is partially hidden behind a holly bush. After crossing another stile on your left, the path becomes more recognisable, almost luxurious by comparison - a wide track between hedges.

This leads you to Lower Hookner. Go through the farmyard, and turn right at the lane. After about 500m there is a T-junction. Turn right, and follow the lane across the Manaton-Moretonhampstead road towards North Bovey. Pass the village sign and where the road curves left at Blackaller, go straight on, up a path signposted to North Bovey village and church. Follow the path round the church, and at the end turn left to go back to the village green and the Ring of Bells or cross the road to the car park.

3. Three Belstone Tales

THE IRISHMAN'S WALL

THE STORIES

For such a small village, Belstone has more than its fair share of folk tales - I have come across three, all of which are said to have taken place within a few kilometres of each other.

The first concerns two Belstone men who were walking across Belstone Common one evening. They had just snared a young hare, and were carrying it home in a net. Suddenly, out of the mist, they heard a loud voice coming from the direction of Cosdon Beacon, to the east. It called mournfully, 'Jacko! Jacko!' On hearing this, the hare leaped up and cried, 'That's me dad!' The men dropped the net in fright, upon which the hare made off in the direction of the Beacon.

This story could be partly ascribed to the effects of the mist and the wind (and probably the local ale!), but the next one is firmly rooted in fact. It concerns the remains of the long wall, called the Irishman's Wall, which can be seen climbing the slopes of Belstone Tor. Under ancient tenement rights, local farmers had the right to enclose up to eight acres of moorland for their own use. Towards the beginning of the nineteenth century, however, a group of Irishmen tried to enclose a much greater area on Belstone Common. Some versions of the story say that they were acting on their own initiative, others that they had been hired by two farmers. What is not in dispute is that they built a wall some 1½ km (almost 1 mile) long. When the local farmers of Belstone and Okehampton parishes saw what was happening, they were outraged, as the resulting enclosure would have severely restricted their access to the moor. They therefore gathered together at the wall, and at a given signal toppled the structure to the ground. The Irishmen departed, never to be seen again, but the parts of the wall that can still be seen bear witness to their skill and determination.

The third tale is much older, and centres on the ring of stones below Belstone Tor known as the Nine Maidens (the Nine Stones on Ordnance Survey maps). The legend says that they are the petrified remains of young girls who had the temerity to dance on the Sabbath, but that is not the end of the story; indeed it is only the beginning. For there are not nine stones, but seventeen. Nine was a magical number in ancient times, and was linked with witchcraft and moon-worship. It is therefore suggested that it was not the Sabbath on which they danced, but the sabbat, the ancient witches' ritual - the word was changed to 'christianise' the story. So they were probably turned to stone either for disturbing a coven of witches, or for practising witchcraft themselves. It is also said that they can still be seen dancing (some say at noon, others at night, at the hunter's moon). Instead of dancing, one version of the story says that all nine stones shift their position very slightly at noon.

THE WALK

Start and Finish: The car park at the entrance to Belstone village. Grid Ref. 621938

Parking: At the car park. There is parking in the village and near the moor gate towards the end of the walk, but it is very limited, and it is only fair to the villagers that visitors should use the car park provided.

Length: 8km (5 miles)

Approximate time: 2$\frac{1}{2}$ hours

Degree of difficulty: B

Route summary: This is a delightful moorland ramble with some outstanding views. There are few clearly defined paths, however, so it is not a walk to be undertaken in poor visibility unless you have the necessary navigational skills. The climb up to Cosdon Beacon is long but fairly easy, but the one up Belstone Tor is steep. One of the river crossings is via a ford, so you should either wear waterproof footwear or be prepared to get your feet wet.

From the car park, turn left into the village. Follow the road as it winds round to the right. Belstone is a delighful little village of mixed thatched and slate-roofed houses. When you come to a telephone box on the right, turn left. You pass the Tors Inn on your right and then, at the edge of the village, turn left again and almost immediately right to follow a track down to the river. This is the Taw, the setting for Harold Williamson's classic *Tarka the Otter*.

The track curves to the left and then to the right to cross the river by a footbridge. Bear right to climb up the other side. This area is a mass of gorse, beautiful when it is in flower. You join a track, bearing right, and then follow it round to the left and up a fairly steep but short slope. When the track peters out, bear half right. You will soon see what looks like a cairn on the skyline. Aim for that. When you get closer, you will find that it is in fact a lone gorse bush. You are on open moorland now, with no path, no trees and few gorse bushes.

If you look back at this point, you will be rewarded with magnificent views across the village and the farmland beyond. There is still no well-defined path, but if you keep in a straight line past the gorse bush, you will soon see Cosdon Hill (called Cawsand Hill by the locals, but Cosdon Hill on the Ordnance Survey map) up ahead, and then you will start climbing through the heather - a carpet of purple in the summer. Keep going in a straight line and you should come to the cairn at Cosdon Beacon. It is a long but relatively easy climb, and the 360 degree views at the top are well worth it. The whole of the northern part of

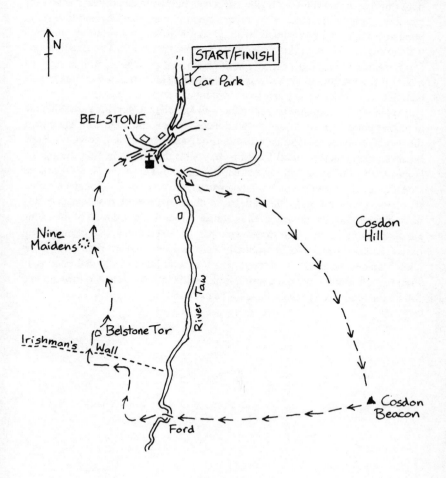

Dartmoor is laid out before you on one side, and the rolling farmland of North Devon on the other.

From Cosdon Beacon turn to the west (the right) and look for the line of the Irishman's Wall climbing up the slope towards Belstone Tor across the valley. Do not aim for the wall, however, but for a point about 400m ($^1/_4$ mile) to the left. This will take you to a ford across the river, which you cannot yet see. Go down the steep, heather-clad slope and then traverse a more level stretch. This part can become a bit waterlogged after rain, but it is relatively easy going, even when it is wet.

When you reach the valley, join the track to cross at the ford in a bend of the river (this means getting your boots or feet wet, but with that proviso it is an easy crossing). Follow the track up the other side to join another one and turn right. Soon you will find the Irishman's Wall on your left. Turn up and follow the path which runs almost alongside as it climbs steeply up the hill. The Belstone and Okehampton farmers did a good demolition job, and most of the wall is now just a line of rubble. But about halfway up, there is a short stretch which is almost complete and which shows just how substantial a structure it was.

At the top, go through the gap in the wall to Belstone Tor, for views that are almost as good as those from Cosdon Beacon. Follow the ridge which connects the two outcrops of rock, and towards the end, bear left, heading downhill. Keep the prominent outcrop called Tor's End to your right, and soon after the ground begins to level off, you will see a small stone circle. This is the Nine Maidens.

Although the use of the number nine when there are actually seventeen stones may have connotations of witchcraft, I am afraid that the word 'maidens' probably has a much more prosaic origin. It is almost certainly a corruption of the Celtic *maen*, meaning 'stone'. The stones were part of the retaining wall of an ancient burial chamber, which would originally have been covered with earth. From the Nine Maidens, bear right to a track, which is soon joined by a wall coming in from the left. Follow the track past a farm on the left to a gate. Go through and follow the road through the village to the car park.

4. Bowerman's Fate

BOWERMAN'S NOSE

THE STORY

In Norman times, there was mighty hunter called Bowerman, who lived in the Manaton area. One day he was out with his hounds when he started a hare. He immediately gave chase and was so engrossed in the hunt that he was not aware that the hare was leading him through a coven of witches in the middle of their ritual.

The witches were incensed, and decided to punish him. So the next time he went out hunting, one of them turned herself into a hare (some versions of the story say a white hare, which because of its rarity would have been especially prized by a keen hunter like Bowerman). She led the poor man a tremendous chase, over the moors and through the valleys, until eventually, when he was well and truly exhausted, she enticed him into an ambush of the other witches. They promptly used their combined powers to turn him into the massive rock now called Bowerman's Nose and his hounds into the rocks at the top of Hound Tor.

THE WALK

Start and Finish: Manaton church. Grid Ref. 750812
Parking: There is a car park on the corner just before the church.
Length: 7km (4½ miles)
Approximate time: 2 hours
Degree of difficulty: B
Route summary: This beautiful route has everything - open moorland, farm fields, woods, riverbanks and lanes - and glorious views into the bargain. It

19

takes you to the strange outcrop that is Bowerman's Nose, then across to where the ill-fated hunter's hounds lie petrified on Hound Tor and back to Manaton, passing through a deserted medieval village on the way. It is relatively easy going, but with a steep climb up to Bowerman's Nose and another, rather less steep, to Hound Tor.

Turn right leaving the car park, and cross the main road to a lane (signposted to Leighon). Follow the lane down between banks and hedges, passing a farm on the right. Just after the farm you begin to climb. Go through the second gate on the right (signposted to Hayne Road for Hayne Down and Jay's Grave).

The path goes diagonally left across a field to a stile. Cross into a lane and turn right. The lane climbs gently and then deteriorates into no more than a track. At the house at the end, bear left up a path, climbing more steeply among some trees, to a gate. Go through it and up to the right, still climbing, with a wall on your right.

As the wall curves away to the right, go straight on through the bracken, aiming for the rocks at the top. You can stop for a breather on the way up and admire the views to the right across to Manaton church and the farmland beyond, and behind you across more of the rolling, variegated fields which are a feature of this north-eastern section of Dartmoor.

As you near the top of the hill, you have to leave the main path and head to the right, still aiming for the rocks at the top. When you reach them, however, curve round to the right below them, to find Bowerman's Nose standing alone on the slope below.

At one time, this rock was believed to be an ancient, man-made idol, and there is no doubt that it bears quite a strong resemblance to the carved stone figures found on Easter Island. However, it is in fact a natural, albeit strangely shaped, formation. Sadly, just as the geologists have proved its physical origins beyond reasonable doubt, so the etymologists have come up with a very prosaic explanation for the origins of the name. It is apparently a corruption of the Celtic *vawr-maen,* meaning simply 'great stone'.

Carry on round the rocks, and more superb views will open up to your right, across to King Tor and Hamel Down. When you get to the opposite side of Hayne Down from the side you came up, head right to join the road below. There is no clearly defined path, but it is very easy to pick your way down through the low gorse. Aim for the point where the road passes through a gate. As you go, the jagged outline of Hound Tor appears on the horizon to the left, with the unmistakable shape of Haytor beyond.

At the road, turn left and go through the gate. Follow the road for about 900m (¹/₂ mile) until it joins a more major road at Swallerton Gate. Turn half left here on to the moor and climb up to Hound Tor. (It is not too strenuous a climb, but if you would rather avoid it, you can skirt round to the left and rejoin the route on the other side.) At the top, turn left to pass through the 'avenue' between the towering rocks. From here you can look back for superb views across the moors and ahead over rolling farmland.

At the end of the 'avenue', bear right and make for the remains of the medieval village which you can just make out in the shadow of Greator Rocks. It is believed that this settlement was abandoned during the Black Death of the fourteenth century, which devastated the population of the area. The ruins of several of the homesteads can still be seen.

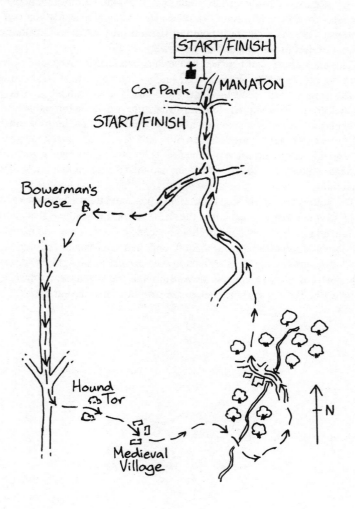

Bear left from the medieval village along a well-worn path to a gate (signposted to Leighon via Haytor Down). Go through it and downhill between fences, with a stand of conifers on the left. Go through another gate and then steeply down to a third, beyond which is the Becka Brook. This is an idyllic spot for a picnic - a beautifully wooded valley with the brook tumbling over the rocks at your feet.

Cross the brook via a stone bridge and then follow the path through the trees on the other side, curving to the right and then to the left. On leaving the trees, turn left (signposted to Leighon), skirting the bottom of Haytor Down. Soon you will find a wall on your left. Follow it to a gate; go through, down a path between two walls and through another gate. Soon afterwards you come to a junction. There is a signpost pointing straight on for the bridlepath, but you should turn left (unsignposted) on to a track.

The track curves left between houses and becomes a tarred lane. Cross the river (still the Becka Brook) by a stone bridge. Ignore the lane which goes off to the left (signposted 'road to Great Houndtor'), and instead go straight on (signposted 'public footpath Houndtor/Manaton road'). Go through a white gate and then turn left over a stile into a wood (signposted 'public footpath'). The path turns to the right, and is marked by yellow waymarks on the trees. Cross a stile and turn left (signposted 'public footpath') still following the waymarks on the trees. Soon you will cross a stream and then a stile on to a track. Turn left into a field.

The yellow waymarks - on rocks, fence posts and trees - continue to indicate the path, which keeps to the left of the field. At the end go through a gate on the left into a lane. Turn right and follow the lane between banks and hedges. You will pass a group of houses on the left, and then see Manaton church ahead of you. At the crossroads by the Manaton village sign, go straight on. After about 200m, on your left, you will pass the gate through which you went at the beginning of the walk. Follow the lane back to the main road and the car park.

5. The Pixie-Led Couple

FICE'S WELL

THE STORY

It is very easy to get lost on Dartmoor, especially when the mist comes down. But although outsiders may believe that it is the mist (and sometimes the ale) which causes people to become disoriented and wander round in circles, the locals know better. It is the pixies who lure the unwary from their path, leading them astray. Hence anyone who is lost is said to be pixie-led.

This is what happened to Sir John Fitz of Tavistock and his wife in Tudor times. They were riding across the moor when the mist came down and the pixies got to work, and before they knew it they were hopelessly lost. The only remedy for those who have been pixie-led is to turn their coats and their pockets inside out, and this is what Sir John and Lady Fitz did. The mist immediately cleared and they discovered that they were by a spring. They refreshed themselves at it and easily found their way home. In gratitude, Sir John had the spring enclosed and covered. His initials 'I.F.' can just be made out on the front of the covering stone, together with the date 1568. The spring is now called Fitz's, or more generally Fice's, Well, 'Fice' being a corruption of 'Fitz'.

Either Sir John made a habit of losing himself or the pixies had a grudge against him, for there is another Fitz's Well, also built by him, near Okehampton! It is said that any young girl who drinks from this second well on Easter morning will be married within a year, but that story can no longer be verified as the spring is now completely covered over.

THE WALK

Start and Finish: The small parking area at the top of the hill just to the east of Merrivale, on the B3357. Grid Ref. 552750

Parking: In the parking area.

Length: 9.5km (6 miles)

Approximate time: $2^1/_2$ hours

Degree of difficulty: A/B

Route summary: Although this is a fairly long walk, it is very easy going, with no steep climbs. Most of it is along well-defined paths, and where it does go across open ground there are clear landmarks to help you identify the route. It is therefore only in thick mist that there is any chance of losing your way. It traces part of the route which Sir John and Lady Fitz would have followed to Fice's Well and also takes in some interesting ancient structures and one superb viewpoint.

Until September 1995, part of this route ventures on to the military range for a short distance (see the detailed route description below), but it is quite safe unless firing is actually taking place. If a red flag is flying from the top of Great Mis Tor when you approach it, then make the slight detour indicated below. If there is no flag, then it is safe to continue. Alternatively, information on times of firing can be obtained from Dartmoor Information Centres. After September 1995 the boundaries of the military range will change, and Great Mis Tor will no longer be a danger area.

Facing away from the road at the parking area, go half left on to the moor. Keep the tall mast on North Hessary Tor to your left, with King's Tor straight ahead. You will come to a well-preserved series of stone rows. The stones are quite small, but it can clearly be seen that there are two double rows running more or less parallel to each other, and to the road, with a third row branching off towards the south-west. There are also stone circles, a kistvaen (a prehistoric burial chamber) and an enormous standing stone over 3m (10ft) high.

It is not clear what purpose these structures served, but it is likely that they had some ritual, perhaps religious, significance in prehistoric times. There are many such rows and circles on Dartmoor, but this is probably the most extensive collection. This area is sometimes called the Plague Market, because farmers used to leave their produce here for the citizens of Tavistock to collect when that town was infected with plague some centuries ago.

At the stone rows, turn left and follow the line of the road, with the North Hessary Tor mast now almost straight ahead. You will pass a stone marker with T on one side and A on the other. This was one of a series which marked the route across the moor. The T indicated the direction to Tavistock and the A the direction to Ashburton. Soon you will pass another car park on your left. Here you should begin to bear left, aiming for the grey pump house on the horizon, and crossing a small leat on the way. Notice the spoil heaps from an old granite quarry on your right. Join the road just before the pump house and turn right.

Follow the road for just over 1km (a little under ³/₄ mile), crossing a cattle grid and passing the turning for Princetown on the right, until you come to a gate with a public footpath sign on the left. Go through the gate, and then through the next one. Follow the track below the wall on the left to a third gate in the wall ahead. There are two more gates ahead, after which you turn right to go through another gate, marked 'access to Fice's Well'. The well is now clearly visible. It is quite a small structure, but interesting, and you should just about be able to make out Sir John Fice's initials and the date etched on the front of the roof, although they are now very weathered.

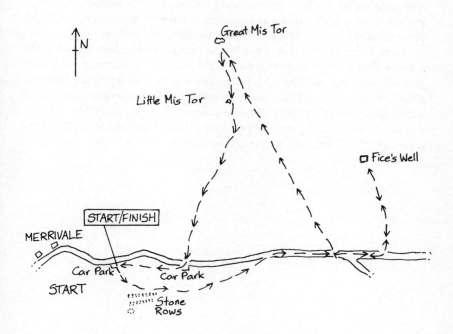

There is unfortunately no public right of way from here on to the moor, so you must retrace your steps along the track and back to the road. Turn right and follow the road in the direction you came from. About 400m ($\frac{1}{4}$ mile) after rejoining the road, you will pass between two almost identical houses, one on each side of the road. Just beyond them, there is a track leading off to the right. It is signposted 'public footpath to the moor', but the signpost is a little way up the track, and is therefore not easily visible from the road.

Go through a gate, and follow the track as it winds between two walls and then on to the open moor. Keep to the wall on the right, and as it gives way to a fence, you will see Great Mis Tor ahead. Until September 1995, you should look for a red flag flying from the pole on the top. If no flag is flying, then carry on up to the tor. If there is a flag, turn left here to join a track which takes you down the hill towards the road. After September 1995 it will be quite safe to visit Great Mis Tor at any time.

The climb up to Great Mis Tor is not difficult, and the views from the top are quite magnificent. You have a 360 degree panorama, with the wild northern moors stretching away to the north and west, gentler farmland to the south-west, and Princetown and more rolling moorland to the south and east.

From Great Mis Tor, turn sharp left and head for Little Mis Tor, the small outcrop of rock a little way to the right of the path you have just come up. Here you will join a track which runs half right towards the road. Merrivale quarry is clearly visible to the right, and you can see Burrator Reservoir in the distance on a clear day. The track curves to the right and joins the road opposite the car park you passed towards the beginning of the walk. Cross the road, turn right and cut across to the parking area from which you started.

6. The Money Pit

THE MONEY PIT

THE STORY

The Money Pit is a kistvaen, an ancient burial chamber, just below Yar Tor. There was once a large stone covering it, topped by a cairn, but both have long since gone.

The tale is told of a farmer from the Poundsgate area, a friendly, open-hearted fellow by all accounts, who had a dream in which he discovered a great hoard of money buried there. Taking this as a sign, he set off as soon as he could and broke into the tomb. He was sadly disappointed, however, for there was nothing there - no human remains and certainly no money. All he could find was a small piece of flint, shaped like a heart. Intrigued by the shape, he decided to take it home, where it sat on his shelf for many a month.

From that day, the farmer underwent a complete change of character. Gone was the sunny, cheerful temperament everyone knew; instead he became sour, churlish and bad tempered. No one could account for the change - it seemed to have happened overnight.

Then one day, about a year later, his son came across the flint on the shelf and took it outside to play with it. As children do, however, he soon lost interest in it and left it lying on the moor. That very same day the farmer reverted to his former good-natured self, and it was only when he discovered that the flint heart had gone from the shelf that he realised why.

THE WALK

Start and finish: Dartmeet. Grid Ref. 672732

Parking: There is a large car park at Dartmeet. However, it is a very popular spot, especially in the summer, so the car park may be full. If so, there is a parking area at the top of the hill to the east, on the road to Ashburton.

Length: 4km (2½ miles)
Approximate time: 1½ hours
Degree of difficulty: A
Links with: Walk 11
Route summary: Apart from the start, in the beautiful Dart valley, this is all moorland walking. We climb Yar Tor for some superb views, then descend to the Money Pit. The route back takes in Sharp Tor, where there is another panoramic view, and another interesting feature of this part of the moor, the Coffin Stone. It is a short walk, along easy-to-follow paths, and there are only two climbs to worry about, one at the beginning and one towards the end.

Dartmeet, as its name suggests, is where the two branches of the River Dart, the East Dart and the West Dart, meet - although the beauty spot of that name is just above the actual confluence. It is a lovely place, with the river (here still the East Dart) flowing by over large boulders, and there is a delightful grassy bank and plenty of trees. Because it is so beautiful, and because there is a large car park, it has become very popular, and on sunny days at weekends you will find a large number of families picnicking there. There is a small kiosk, some toilets, and beyond the car park a rather nice restaurant and café complex.

Our walk starts at the end of the car park. Instead of following the drive up to the restaurant, bear right through a kissing gate to climb gently away from the river. On the way, you will pass an interesting collection of birds on your left - peacocks, exotic pheasants and a number of other colourful breeds.

Just beyond the cages, branch off to the right to climb up towards Yar Tor. It is initially quite steep, but it becomes less so a little higher up. The path is easy to follow and the going is not too rough. There are also plenty of rocks along the way on which you can sit while you catch your breath, looking back over the river to a lovely view of the patchwork of fields on the other side, stretching up to the open moors and hills in the distance.

When you reach the top, of course, the views are even more outstanding - to the north a mixture of farms and moorland, to the south a rolling landscape of tors and hills and to the west the lovely Dart valley. Only to the east is the outlook somewhat obscured by Corndon Tor.

From Yar Tor a path leads towards the south-east (half right from the path you came up on) towards a cross you can see on the other side of the road. Follow it and just before you reach the road, you will see a small circle of stones on the right, inside which is a shallow dip and what looks like a small collapsed entrance. These are the remains of the Money Pit.

At this point, it might be worth taking a short detour across the road to investigate the cross on the other side. It is not one of the ancient crosses which one finds scattered across the moor, but was erected earlier this century as a memorial to Lt Cave Penney, a member of a local family, who died in Palestine towards the end of the First World War at the tender age of nineteen.

Turn right from the Money Pit to follow the road. (If you are not keen on road walking, there are plenty of paths which follow the rough line of the road.) You should be aiming for Sharp Tor, which is clearly visible across the main road ahead. It is appropriately named - from here it has a very angular appearance.

Cross the road and follow the broad, clearly defined and easy path up to the tor. There is an easy climb up to the top, and the views from there are, if anything, better than those from Yar Tor, with the Dart valley winding down to the south-east, and the same rolling moors and hills to the south and west.

Turn back towards the road, but instead of following the broad path back, bear left down a narrower one to go down into the valley below. At the bottom, you will pass an enclosure on your right (to which there is no public access), which contains the ruins of an old farmstead. Over to the left, lower down the valley, is Rowbrook Farm, the scene of another Dartmoor legend, that of Jan Coo.

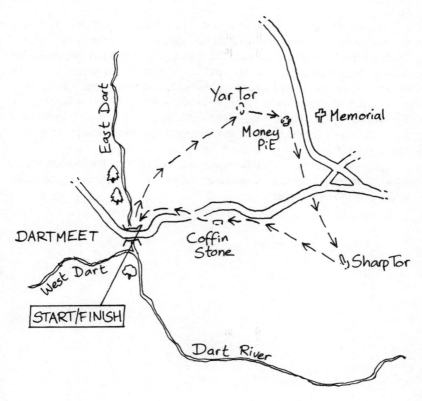

Jan was an orphan who worked on the farm. One evening he heard a voice coming from the River Dart, which is on the other side of the farm. It was calling, 'Jan Coo, Jan Coo.' He called some of the farm labourers, who also heard it, and answered. The voice immediately stopped. They searched the area, but found nothing. The same thing happened the next night, and the men decided that it was the pixies up to no good.

It was some months later that the voice was next heard, and this time Jan himself answered. Instead of the voice stopping, it called again. Jan decided that he would go and find out for himself who was calling. He ran down to the river and was never seen again. Some say he was spirited away by the pixies, others that it was the Dart itself calling, and that it was the river that claimed him.

From the enclosure, follow the clear path which goes up the other side of the valley. Take it gently, as the last short stretch is steep. It brings you out near the parking area at the top of the hill above Dartmeet. Turn left along the grassy track which follows the line of the road. Where the road takes a wide arc to the right, you will come across another interesting feature of the area, the Coffin Stone.

In the Middle Ages, when someone died in the Dart valley, their coffin had to be carried to Widecombe on foot for burial - there was no transport on the moor. The funeral cortège would rest here after the steep climb from the clapper bridge at Dartmeet, and the large rock was a convenient place for the bearers to rest the coffin. When they resumed the journey, one of the mourners would carve a cross or the deceased's initials on the rock, and some of these can still be faintly seen. You will see that the stone is split in two. It is said that one day the coffin of a particularly wicked person was rested here, and that both it and the rock were struck by lightning.

Cross the road from the Coffin Stone, and start working your way downhill towards the river. Cross a track and bear right to reach the kissing gate which leads back into the car park.

7. Ephraim's Pinch

WIDECOMBE CHURCH

THE STORY

Ephraim's Pinch is a short hill on the southern edge of Soussons Plantation. As with many Dartmoor tales, the story of how it got its name has different versions. The most common, and probably the most authentic, dates back to at least the beginning of the last century and probably earlier, and tells of a young Widecombe man called Ephraim who was renowned for his strength.

One day, for a bet, he undertook to carry a sack of corn on his back all the way from Widecombe to Postbridge, a distance of about 10km (6 miles), without putting it down. He duly set off and was going well as he crossed Rowden Hill. But by the time he reached the West Webburn River he was tiring fast, and the short hill a little further on proved too much for him. He threw the sack to the ground in disgust and lost his bet, but the hill was named Ephraim's Pinch to commemorate his feat in getting as far as he did.

Another, more romanticised and probably more modern, version says that he carried the sack of corn to prove to his sweetheart's father that he had the strength and stamina to be a fitting suitor for his daughter. In this version, the strain of climbing the hill was too great for him and he collapsed and subsequently died of his injuries.

THE WALK

Start and finish: Widecombe in the Moor. Grid Ref. 718768.

Parking: There is a free car park at the eastern end of the village green, opposite the church. If this is full (as it might well be on a sunny summer weekend), there is a pay car park next to the kiosk at the other end of the green.

Length: 12km (7¹/₂ miles)

Approximate time: 3 - 3¹/₂ hours

Degree of difficulty: B

Links with: Walks 1 and 17

Route summary: We follow Ephraim's probable route from Widecombe to Ephraim's Pinch, and return across moorland and along pretty lanes. It is a delightful walk through some lovely countryside, with extensive views from the higher ground. It is mainly along paths, tracks and quiet little roads, and apart from one steep climb up from Widecombe to the edge of Hamel Down, none of the hills is unduly difficult.

Widecombe is an attractive little village with a lovely old church whose tall tower has earned it the nickname the Cathedral of the Moor. It is very popular with visitors, partly because of its beauty and partly because of the famous song 'Widecombe Fair'. Because of this popularity, it boasts several gift shops and cafés. The sixteenth-century Church House is owned by the National Trust.

Turn right outside the car park and follow the path alongside the green. At the end turn right past the kiosk and the pay car park. After about 100m, you will find a lane on your left, signposted 'Path to Hameldown for Grimspound'. Follow it as it climbs steeply between two walls, and at the end follow the narrow, stony track which leads straight on.

Go through the gate at the end, out onto the open moor, and carry straight on, following the line of the wall on your right. At the top corner of the wall, there is a fingerpost pointing back down to Widecombe. Bear right onto a track. There is a gorgeous view to your right as you follow the track, over Widecombe and the lush green fields around it to the range of tors beyond.

You will pass another fingerpost, also pointing back the way you have come, and just after it, where your track crosses another, go straight on, heading away from the wall. Another view now appears, this time ahead and to your left across fields and plantations, with the mast on North Hessary Tor, above Princetown, standing out in the distance.

The track begins to descend gently. It meets the corner of a wall and continues along to the right of it. Soon you will see a gate through the wall on your left, signposted simply 'path'. Turn through it and follow the path which leads down between gorse-covered walls. This is a pretty stretch, with a mass of yellow on either side of you and rolling views ahead. The path goes down to another gate and then to a stile which leads to the road at Blackaton Cross.

Go straight across and follow the road down to cross a stream. It climbs gently up the other side of the valley, curving to left and right as it goes, and then begins to descend again. Although these hills are not as steep as the initial climb out of Widecombe, one can imagine how the constant ups and downs of the road must have sapped poor Ephraim's strength. Look out for rabbits along here, as the banks and fields along this stretch of the road are teeming with them.

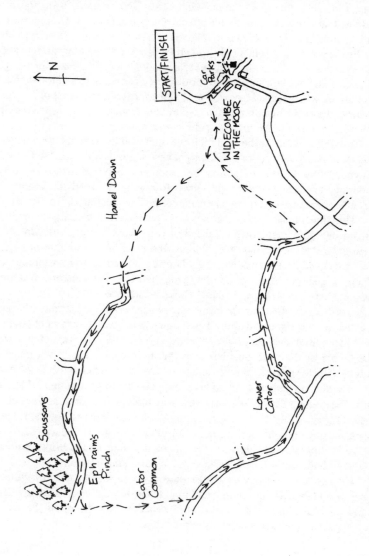

As the road levels off again, you pass a turn-off to the right. Keep straight on (signposted to Postbridge and Princetown) and cross the West Webburn River. The road starts to climb gently again, passing the attractive granite Grendon Cottage on the left.

Soussons Plantation now appears on your right. You cross a cattle grid and start climbing gently again, with a mass of purple heather stretching away to the plantation. Cross another cattle grid, and you are on Ephraim's Pinch. The hill seems too short and gentle to have defeated Ephraim on its own, so one must assume that it was the cumulative effects of the distance and the numerous small hills and valleys that forced him to give up.

Just beyond the second cattle grid you will see a track going straight ahead as the road curves to the right. Follow it for about 300m until you come to a gate in the fence on your left, signposted 'bridlepath'. Turn in here and follow the well-worn track which leads across Cator Common. After a kilometre or so (just over $^1/_2$ mile) it meets a line of trees which comes in from the left. Keep to the right of the trees and follow the line to a gate on to a road.

Turn left and follow the road. It is pleasant walking without too much traffic, and there is a lovely outlook to the right as you go. Pass the road to Cator Court on your left and carry straight on. You soon pass between two stone posts, and moorland opens up on your right. Keep following the road for another 400m ($^1/_4$ mile) or so, until you see an unsignposted lane leading off to the left.

Turn down it and follow it as it winds down past Lower Cator Farm, with the great ridge of Hamel Down up ahead of you. Cross a pretty little stream at the bottom, and climb up the other side. At the junction, go straight on. The road descends gently between banks of wild flowers and gorse to cross another stream. There is a short climb up the other side, and then it levels off. You are now walking between walls, and Hamel Down is half left.

Pass the beautiful thatched farmhouse which is now the Dartmoor Expedition Centre on your right, and at the T-junction just beyond it, turn right (signposted to Widecombe). Pass through a gateway with no gate, and after a few metres, at the corner of the wall, turn left onto the moor again. There is a magnificent rolling vista to your left, of fields and woods, with a number of tors in the distance.

There is no path as such up here, but you should be aiming half left up the hill. The going is easy as you pick your way through the gorse, and although it is a fairly long climb, it is not very steep. As you reach the top of the ridge, look back and to your right for some quite outstanding views, all the way across South Devon behind you and across to the tors on the other side of Widecombe on the right, with the unmistakeable shape of Haytor on the horizon.

Then as you come down the other side, you will see the tower of Widecombe church, and then a wall running downhill towards the village. This is where you came up. Make for the fingerpost at the corner of the wall, follow the path down to the gate and retrace your steps to the village and the car park.

8. The Top Hat

HOOTEN WHEALS

THE STORY

Dartmoor's mires are places to be approached with caution; they have an awesome reputation, and many a tale has been told of how unwary travellers have come to grief in them. Although Aune Head Mires are not quite as notorious as, say, Fox Tor Mires, they should still be treated with the greatest respect, as the following popular and delightful - if rather unlikely - story illustrates.

A young man was passing through the area, picking his way gingerly across the mires, when he came across a top hat lying in the water. He looked at it for some time, wondering how someone had come to leave such a splendid piece of headgear lying around, and then, being of an irreverent turn of mind, he gave it a hefty kick.

'Hey,' said a voice from beneath it. 'What be you a-doin' to my 'at?'

The young man jumped back in surprise, and looked at the hat with renewed interest. 'Be there someone under'n then?' he asked.

''Ess, I reckon so,' said the voice. 'An' a hoss under me an' all!'

The tale generally ends there, leaving us to wonder what became of the owner of the hat. Some more modern versions try to correct this omission, however, by going on to recount how the young man rescued not only him but his horse as well - and all single-handed!

THE WALK

Start and finish: There is a small track leading off the road between Venford Reservoir and Hexworthy, about 200m east of the Forest Inn, signposted to Sherberton. The walk starts and finishes at the top of that track, about 400m (¼ mile) from the turn-off. Grid Ref. 652726

Parking: Alongside the track by the public bridlepath sign which leads off to the left.

Length: 6.5km (4 miles)

Approximate time: 2 hours

Degree of difficulty: B

Links with: Walk 11

Route summary: This is a wild, open stretch of the moor, with few outstanding features. It nevertheless has a strange, almost eerie attraction all its own - the beauty of seemingly endless space, distant horizons and immense skies. The impression of desolation is somewhat deceptive, however, as there are farms and settlements not far to the north, east and west. There are excellent views as you go, particularly to the north and west. The route takes you across this great expanse to Aune Head Mires and back via some interesting old tin mines. There are no steep climbs and the going is relatively easy for most of the walk, apart from one or two tussocky stretches. But there are virtually no paths and few landmarks, so it should not be attempted in poor visibility.

Follow the bridlepath through the gate, but then leave it to bear left and walk across the open moor between the two stone walls, aiming for the far corner of the one on your right. As you go, you will be able to enjoy lovely views to Royal Hill and the tors around Princetown on your right and to the northern moors behind you. When you reach the corner of the wall, carry on up the hill, trying to keep to a straight line.

Before you have gone very far, you will see your next landmark, a valley (called Deep Swincombe) stretching up from the right. Aim for the valley head, which should be almost straight ahead. Pass it and carry on, keeping to your straight line. Here the ground becomes a little less easy, with tussocks of grass to negotiate, and it can become a little damp underfoot. These conditions do not last for too long, however, and at no time is the going very difficult.

Once again you will find yourself temporarily without something to aim for, but keep to your straight line and soon Ter Hill will appear up ahead, with a cross clearly visible on the horizon. Aim for that cross. The ascent is still very gentle, and it becomes somewhat easier underfoot as you go. The cross is an old route marker, one of several that were erected to show the route of the Abbots' Way, the ancient track that linked the abbey of Buckfast on the south-eastern edge of the moor with those of Tavistock and Buckland to the west. The views from up here are quite superb, with the moors rolling away seemingly endlessly behind you.

Turn left at the cross, and traverse a stretch of country which is remarkably featureless. There are virtually no reference points, and yet the desolation of the place simply seems to add to its appeal. And the silence is immense, broken only by the singing of the larks from time to time. After about 600m ($^1/_3$ mile), Skir Gut will appear on your left. Pass the top of the gully and soon a shallow valley will be seen disappearing into the distance ahead. This is the beginning of the River Avon, and the expanse of rushes, sedge, moss and water in front of it is Aune Head Mires - so called because they mark the head of the Avon, 'Aune' being a corruption of 'Avon'.

Turn sharp left to skirt round the edge of the mires, making sure that you avoid the marshy stretches. Head directly away from them, and from the Avon valley behind them, keeping the slopes of Ryder's Hill to your right - this means that you will be going more or less north. Magnificent views of the northern

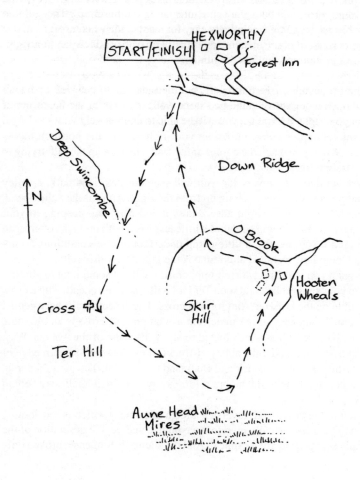

moors open up again, this time ahead of you, and the whole area is a mass of purple heather in the summer. Look out for the occasional grouse - not a very common sight, but one to be appreciated if you are fortunate enough.

After about 300m, you will come across a stream flowing away northwards ahead of you. Keep to the left bank as you follow it down. About 500m (just over $\frac{1}{4}$ mile) from the head of the stream, you will come to the ruins of Hooten Wheals tin mine. This mine, part of a larger complex known as Hexworthy Mines, was in production right up until the early part of this century, although looking at it now, that is hard to believe as there is so little left. But there are interesting gullies and spoil heaps to see, and the remains of the dressing floors.

Turn left here and take the path and then the track which follow the valley of the strangely named O Brook. Keep to the track as it veers left away from the brook to climb gently up the valley side. It ends at another deep gully - all that remains of Hensroost Mine, another in the Hexworthy Mines complex.

There is no easily recognisable path from Hensroost, but if you turn right, you can make your way across the tussocks to cross the brook. Once across, carry straight on up the gentle slope on the other side, and as you reach the top of Down Ridge, the view to the north will open up again. Soon you will see a wall running across the bottom of the ridge ahead of you. Aim for the left-hand corner and follow the wall back to the bridlepath, the gate and the road.

9. The Gubbins of Lydford Gorge

THE WHITE LADY

THE STORY

The Gubbins were a family of red-haired outlaws and robbers who terrorised the western part of Dartmoor some centuries ago. Many murders were attributed to them, and they were even said to be cannibals. Their home was in Lydford Gorge, where Thomas Fuller, writing in the seventeenth century, described them as living 'in cots (rather holes than houses) like swine, having all in common, multiplied without marriage into many hundreds'. Visiting the gorge, even today, it is easy to understand how difficult it must have been to track them down and bring them to justice, especially as they had the reputation of being able to outrun a horse.

They appear in Charles Kingsley's novel *Westward Ho!* Set in Tudor times, it describes how a party of travellers from Okehampton to Tavistock wore helmets and breastplates and carried their arms at the ready as they crossed this part of the moor, for fear of being attacked by the Gubbins. They stopped overnight at the Dartmoor Inn, which still stands on the main road just opposite the turn-off for Lydford, and it was there that the Gubbins tried to surprise them. The travellers beat them off, and one of Kingsley's characters, Salvation Yeo, killed their 'king'.

The clan was gradually civilised and became absorbed into the local community, but it is believed that the Doones in R.D. Blackmore's classic *Lorna Doone* were modelled on them.

THE WALK

Start and finish: The main entrance to Lydford Gorge. Grid Ref. 509845
Parking: There is a large car park at the entrance.
Length: 5km (3 miles)
Approximate time: 1½ hours
Degree of difficulty: A
Route summary: This is a stunningly beautiful circuit of Lydford Gorge which takes you along the top of the almost vertical ravine, then back along the banks of the River Lyd. It is generally fairly easy, and the path is very well marked, but there are some fairly steep sections - although even these are made less difficult by the provision of steps and occasionally handrails. Down by the river there are some narrow paths which can become slippery when wet, so care is needed on those sections.

Lydford Gorge is a National Trust property, so there is a small entrance fee for non-members. Note too that this walk is only possible from 1 April to 31 October - during the winter months, there is access only from the southern entrance to the White Lady waterfall, for safety reasons.

Pay your entrance fee (or show your National Trust membership card) at the entrance, and then follow the path which leads down to a sign saying 'Way in'. Once in the gorge proper, the path zigzags down and then follows the side of the steep, narrow ravine. You can hear the River Lyd babbling away, and occasionally see it, below you on the right.

You come to a T-junction, at which you should turn left (signposted to the waterfall entrance). This path winds away from the gorge for a stretch, with masses of wild flowers on either side. You go up some steps, and then get a view of the river far below. The path winds away from the gorge again, climbing as it goes, but again the going is made easier by some steps. At the top is a bench on which you can sit and admire the outlook.

Just beyond the bench, you get a view across to the moors on the left to complement the one down through the mixed woodland to the river on the right. You cross a wooden footbridge and go up a few more steps and then start to descend, still amongst a carpet of wild flowers. Cross another footbridge, climb a few steps and then begin to descend in earnest, again with some steps to make the going easier. There are trees on both sides of the path now, and the place is usually alive with birdsong.

The path levels off again and then climbs quite steeply (with steps again, and with another bench at the top on which to sit and catch your breath). Soon after the bench, turn right to cross a footbridge and then left up a gentle climb. At the top, go right to continue the walk (signposted to the White Lady waterfall) or straight on if you want refreshments or toilets (signposted 'Way out and refreshments').

About 100m or so after the signpost, you have a choice as the path forks. You can go right for a shorter but steeper route down to the river, with steps and a handrail, or left along an easier route, but one that adds about 15 minutes to the walk. I would recommend the shorter route for anyone of average fitness, as it is not too steep a descent, and the steps and handrail help.

The two routes come together again at the spectacular White Lady waterfall - a virtually sheer drop of about 27m (90ft). It is a gorgeous spot, with the water cascading down and the sunlight sparkling on the river below. There is a legend associated with the waterfall to the effect that if anyone falls into the river here and sees a woman in white, they will not drown.

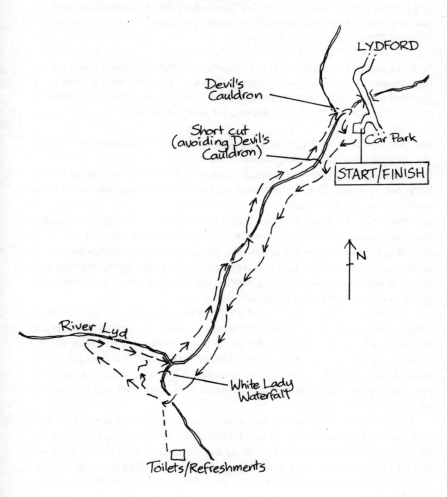

The path curves to the left below the waterfall, crosses a wooden footbridge and then goes right to follow the river upstream, hugging the bank. It is quite lovely along here, but you should proceed with care, as the path is rocky and therefore slippery when wet. You climb up the side of the ravine for a short stretch (again with steps) and then the path levels off. The river is still visible (and very definitely audible) down on the right, with the sun dappling the surface as it filters through the trees.

The path soon rejoins the river, and meanders alongside it. It is an idyllic stretch, with the water chattering beside you, the birds singing in the woods above you and the wild flowers all around. You pass under an overhanging rock and then turn right on to a footbridge across the river. This leads to a wooden walkway, with the river rushing down beside it in a series of stunning cascades. You cross back to the other side of the river, go through a short tunnel in the rock and follow the rock path. Take care, as it is very narrow in places, although there is a handrail to hold on to. There are one or two short climbs, but the path is generally level. Soon both the path and the river broaden out, and then you come to a footbridge on the right. Go straight on if you want to visit the Devil's Cauldron. The path becomes quite steep, however (although there are the usual steps and handrail), and at particularly busy times there can be up to an hour's wait to view the Cauldron itself, so if you want to by-pass it turn right over the footbridge for a short cut back to the car park.

Otherwise keep on until the path turns right to cross a concrete footbridge higher up, and then goes left along the side of the gorge. You have to leave the main path for the short walk to the Devil's Cauldron itself, and only six people are allowed down at any one time. But it is an exciting sight as the water rushes through a narrow gap in the rock and boils around the pool below.

When you have visited the Devil's Cauldron, continue up the main path (signposted 'way out') and at the junction turn sharp right (signposted 'way out' again). At the top of this path is a picnic area. You turn left (signposted to the main entrance and shop) to return to the car park.

10. The Evil Squire Cabell

SQUIRE CABELL'S
TOMB

THE STORY

Richard Cabell was a particularly wicked squire who lived in the seventeenth century. His evil reputation was such that he was even said to have sold his soul to the Devil. When he died in 1677, he was buried under an enormous stone slab to keep him in his grave and a special building was constructed around the tomb to make doubly sure.

He was a great huntsman, and it is said that when he was buried, a pack of black phantom hounds came howling round the tomb - and that they return on dark, stormy nights. Some accounts say that the Devil's imps gather at the tomb from time to time to try to carry away the squire's soul, others that his ghost comes out and can be seen hunting with his black dogs along the Abbots' Way, the ancient track running from Buckfast Abbey across the moor to Tavistock. According to this account, if you see him out hunting, you will die within a year.

Sir Arthur Conan Doyle, the creator of Sherlock Holmes, used to visit Dartmoor regularly, and the story of Squire Cabell and his hounds served as the inspiration for one of his greatest novels, *The Hound of the Baskervilles*.

THE WALK

Start and finish: Holy Trinity Church, Buckfastleigh. Grid Ref. 743665
Parking: At the end of the lane up to the church.
Length: 12.5km (7³⁄₄ miles)

Approximate time: $3^1/_2$ hours
Degree of difficulty: B
Route summary: This walk takes us from Squire Cabell's tomb at Buckfastleigh to the scene of his phantom hunt at the start of the Abbots' Way, and then back via the beautiful Dean Wood. Most of the route is along quiet country lanes but there are some moorland and farm paths in the middle. It passes through varied scenery - farms, woods and open moorland - and there are one or two breathtaking views. The going is easy, with few steep climbs and little chance of going wrong.

The church at Buckfastleigh was destroyed by fire in 1992, and only the gutted ruins remain. The churchyard is still open, however, and you can see the remains of a thirteenth-century chantry chapel at one end. The square bulk of Squire Cabell's tomb is just opposite the entrance porch of the church itself. The churchyard is on the edge of a very steep cliff, looking out over Buckfast, so the view northwards is superb.

Turn right outside the churchyard and follow the lane up which you drove, with the view across to the magnificent Buckfast Abbey to your right. At the fork go right and climb gently between banks of wild flowers. At the crossroads, go straight on (signposted to Holne and Scorriton). Where another road goes off to the right, go straight on (still signposted to Scorriton and Holne). It is easy, level walking, with pleasant views of fields and woods and banks of flowers on either side.

Pass Five Oaks Cross (still following the signpost to Holne), and about 100m further on, at Hockmoorhead, turn left into a pretty little lane (signposted to Bowden and Cross Furzes). This takes you downhill, with a view of woods and moors ahead, to cross a small stream. You soon pass an attractive old farmhouse on the right, with some gorgeous rhododendrons in the garden.

The lane curves to the right after the farmhouse and climbs into a delightful, cool wood. It is a steep climb at first, but eases off further on. It is beautifully peaceful along here, and usually the only sound you can hear is the birdsong. At the top of the rise, the woods give way to fields and you pass Button Farm on the left. You soon continue climbing, past Parkland Farm on the right. It is not a very steep ascent, but it is quite long.

The lane curves to the right and levels off somewhat. Pause when you come to a break in the hedge on the right to admire the lovely view across a patchwork of fields to the hills in the distance. You pass Bowerdon Farm on the left and then start to climb gently again. The silence is almost tangible, and even the birds seem to be reluctant to break it up here.

At the top, look right again for another stunning view. The open moor, clad in gorse, lies straight ahead. Carry on to the junction at Cross Furzes, and go straight across the road to a track (signposted 'Abbots' Way bridlepath to Plym

Ford' and 'bridlepath to Moor Cross').

The track descends steeply among the trees to a ford, with a small clapper footbridge alongside. This is a lovely spot to stop for a picnic or just for a rest alongside the stream. Go through the gate on the other side of the ford and turn left (signposted 'bridlepath to Moor Cross'). A rough track climbs through the gorse and then passes through a gap in a bank. You can look across the deep,

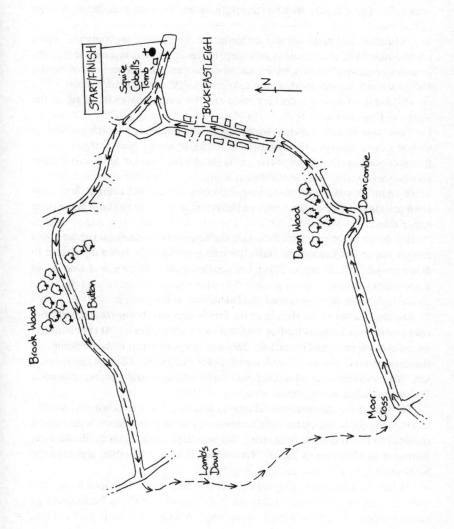

wooded valley to the rolling farmland beyond on your left, and behind you the moors stretch away into the distance.

The track curves to the right, away from the valley, and becomes less distinct, but still recognisable. You pass a stand of majestic old beech trees on your right and then go through another gap in a bank and bear left to a gate. The ground around the gate can be very muddy after rain, so be careful. Pass through the gate and turn left to follow a wall and fence, still with the same superb view to your left. This stretch can be a bit soggy underfoot after rain, but it is quite passable.

When the wall takes a dog's leg to the left, go straight on, to meet it again about 150m further on. A new panorama opens up now, stretching far into the distance ahead, with gently rolling moorland to the right. When you rejoin the wall, cross it via a stile next to a gate, and bear right (signposted 'path').

This is the only place where the route might become a little confusing, as the signpost does not show the direction of the bridlepath very clearly. You should keep the fence on your left, but strike slightly away from it rather than following its line as the signpost would suggest. You will soon see a stile next to a gate in the fence ahead of you. Cross it and go diagonally across the next field to another gate and stile which lead onto a track.

Turn left into the track and follow it down until it meets a tarred lane. Turn left here (signposted to Skerraton), and follow a long lane edged with hedgerows full of flowers. After about 2km (1 $\frac{1}{4}$ miles) it curves sharp right and goes quite steeply down to Deancombe. Turn left at Deancombe and follow the lane as it curves down through Dean Wood to cross the Dean Burn. This is a lovely stretch of road, with the trees meeting overhead and the stream tumbling down alongside you on the right.

All too soon, you leave the wood - and the stream - and begin to hear, and then to see, the busy A38 ahead of you. The lane climbs briefly to a crossroads. Go straight ahead (signposted to Buckfastleigh) and soon you pass the backs of the houses on the outskirts of Buckfastleigh on your right. At the junction go straight on into Duckspond Road, with a football pitch on your right. At the next junction go straight on again. Do not take the turning to the right signposted to the town centre, but keep on down a very narrow lane.

You come out opposite the Waterman's Arms. Cross the road into Market Street. This street runs into Bridge Street, which soon becomes Church Street and leads out of the town. As it curves to the left, go straight on up Church Hill. There is a steady climb up the hill to a junction at the top. Go right to get back to the church.

11. The Haunting of Hangman's Pit

HANGMAN'S PIT

THE STORY

Samuel Hannaford was a farmer who lived at Round Hill, not far from Two Bridges. One day in 1826 he went to Brent Fair where, according to some versions of the story, he exchanged his horse for another, which turned out to be lame. Other versions say that he sold his horse, got drunk on the proceeds and then bought the same horse back again for a greatly increased price.

Either way, he was so worried about what he had done, and how his wife would react when he told her, that he stopped at a deep gully on the way home and hanged himself from one of the rowan trees growing there. It is said that his wife swore she saw (or in some versions of the story only heard) him arriving home at exactly the time of his suicide.

The place where he died has been called Hangman's Pit ever since. It lies about 300m south-east of Combestone Tor on the road from Holne to Hexworthy, and legend has it that his ghost can sometimes be seen visiting the hollow at midnight, then riding off in the direction of Round Hill.

THE WALK

Start and finish: Hangman's Pit, a small gully about 300m from Combestone Tor and about 1km ($1/2$ mile) from Venford Reservoir on the Holne-Hexworthy road. It is beside the road on the northern side (the right as you come from Holne). Grid Ref. 672715

Parking: There is a car park at Combestone Tor.

Length: 5.5km ($3^1/2$ miles)

Approximate time: 1 - 2 hours

Degree of difficulty: A

Links with: Walks 6 and 8

Route summary: This walk takes you from Hangman's Pit along part of the route of Samuel Hannaford's ghost on its way to Round Hill, and then doubles back across farm fields and open moorland. It incorporates some lovely riverside walking as well as breathtaking scenery, and is all relatively easy, with only a few gentle climbs. It is not a walk to do after heavy rain however: halfway through, you have to negotiate stepping stones across the West Dart River, and although they are very easy to manage most of the time, they can become difficult when the river is in spate.

From Hangman's Pit, follow the road towards Hexworthy, past Combestone Tor, down the hill, across a bridge and cattle grid and then up the other side. There is a taste of what is in store for you in the views across the river to your right.

At the junction, go straight on (signposted to Princetown) and down another hill, twisting first to the right and then to the left. Near the bottom you pass the Forest Inn on your left. Follow the road round to the right (signposted to Princetown again), and then as it curves left, notice the house on the left-hand side, called Jolly Lane Cot. It has an interesting history: it was the last house in Devon to be built according to an ancient tradition which laid down that anyone who could enclose a piece of land, build a house on it and light a fire inside in one day between sunrise and sunset became the legal owner.

One day in 1835, when the farmers who held ancient tenants' rights to the land in the area were at Ashburton Fair, a man called Tom Satterley, with the help of the local labourers, set about enclosing the land and building the house, and by the time the fair had ended and the farmers returned, the fire was lit. The cottage's appearance has changed somewhat over the years, especially with the addition of a second storey early this century and the replacement of the thatch with slates, but it is not too difficult to imagine the simple cottage that it once was.

Follow the road round to the right, cross the stream below and continue among the trees alongside it, and then alongside the rather wider West Dart River. The road continues to wind first to the left and then to the right, and crosses the river via a beautiful stone bridge. The river is now on your left, but soon it curves away while the road goes straight on up a hill.

You pass a church on your right, and soon afterwards, the road curves to the left. Turn right here up a track. After a few metres turn left (signposted to Dartmeet) and go through a gate into a field. Cross the field, following the yellow stakes which mark the path. At the top of the rise there is a footpath sign, and you look straight ahead to Yar Tor above the popular picnic spot of Dartmeet. There are also extensive views behind you.

Continue to follow the yellow stakes (and yellow dots painted on the odd rocks) down the field to a gap in the wall on the right (signposted to Dartmeet). This leads you onto a path between walls, still with yellow dots painted on the rocks to show that you are on the right route. Cross a stile and continue down between two walls to a gateway on the left, marked with a yellow dot on each stone post.

Go through the gateway and follow the yellow stakes across the field beyond, down towards the house at the bottom. When you get there, go right (signposted 'bridlepath to Combestone via stepping stones'). This takes you down to the river and the stepping stones. These are usually quite dry and easy to negotiate, but after heavy rain they can become wet or even completely covered by water. If they do happen to be covered, then it is best not to risk trying to cross and your only alternative is to return the way you came.

Once across the river, go straight on up the hill and into the trees to a gap in the wall ahead (marked with a blue waymark). Go through and follow the line of trees on your left. Go through the gap in the next wall and keep straight on, now with a wall on your left. Cross a track and carry straight on (signposted 'bridlepath Holne road at Combestone Tor'). At the top, your view is dominated by tors on all sides: to the left, down the Dart valley is Aish Tor; behind you is Yar Tor; to the right lie Bellever Tor, Longaford Tor and the mast on North Hessary Tor; and ahead you can now see Combestone Tor and the rolling moorland beyond.

The track you are on crosses a cattle grid and then curves left to another (signposted 'bridlepath Holne road at Combestone Tor' again). Bear left off the track to climb up to Combestone Tor for the best views of all. You can see down the Dart valley and beyond across moors and fields to the east and over an almost endless expanse of moorland and woods to the north and west. The tors you can now see are too numerous to list here; suffice it to say that the panorama is quite stunning.

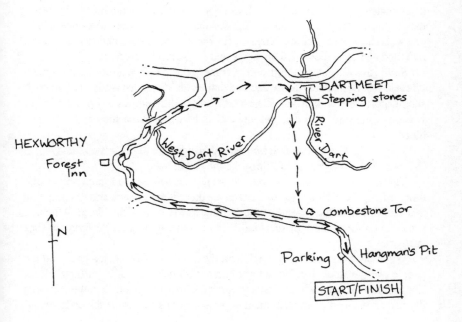

12. Childe the Hunter

CHILDE'S TOMB

THE STORY

The well-known Dartmoor landmark known as Childe's Tomb is badly named: the man it commemorates was not called Childe, and it is not his tomb.

The story of the man who has come to be known as 'Childe the Hunter' dates back to the time of the Norman Conquest. A Saxon nobleman or *cild* (hence the corruption 'childe') called Ordulf was out hunting on the moors one winter day when he was caught in a blizzard. He was forced to stop, and to keep warm, he killed and disembowelled his horse and crept into its carcass.

Sadly, this did not save him, and he froze to death before he could be rescued. It is said that he had previously decreed that on his death, his lands in Plymstock should go to the church where he was buried, although a more romanticised version of the story says that before he died, he wrote in the snow in his horse's blood:

> They fyrste that fyndes and brings mee to my grave,
> The priorie of Plimstoke they shall have.

These lines were also said to have been inscribed on the tomb itself at one time, although there is no sign of them on the present monument, and it is probable that this is where the legend of the writing in the snow came from. After all, someone on the point of death is unlikely to bother to express his dying wishes in rhyme!

When his body was discovered, both the monks of Tavistock Abbey and the people of Plymstock decided to bury him and so gain his lands for themselves. The monks reached the body first and carried it back to Tavistock, but the men of Plymstock decided to ambush them at the only bridge over the River Tavy and steal it from them. On hearing of this ploy, the monks improvised a new bridge further upstream, and so got the body safely to the Abbey and claimed Ordulf's lands.

There is a further twist to the tale: some people claim that a procession of phantom monks has been seen emerging from the mist in the area, accompanied by the sound of chanting.

THE WALK

Start and finish: High Moorland Visitor Centre, Princetown. Grid Ref. 590735
Parking: There is a pay car park behind the Visitor Centre.
Length: 13.5km (8½ miles)
Approximate time: 3½ - 4 hours
Degree of difficulty: B
Route summary: This superb walk gives you a taste of the high moor without too much effort, and you are seldom without an extensive view. It is a circular route from Princetown to Childe's Tomb and back, and is relatively undemanding, although you will find stout shoes useful in negotiating some of the rougher ground. Along the way you come across the oldest recorded cross on the moor, a feat of eighteenth-century engineering and the bog that inspired Sir Arthur Conan Doyle's *The Hound of the Baskervilles*.

I have suggested starting this walk at the High Moorland Visitor Centre because it is well worth visiting before you set off. It provides a fascinating exposition of the high moor, including its history, wildlife and people, and the activities that take place there today, all in a series of displays, exhibitions and films. It is a very good introduction to this unique landscape and its background, and there is no entrance fee.

To start the walk, turn right outside the Visitor Centre and cross the road to the Plume of Feathers Inn. Take the lane that runs alongside the pub, between it and the Devil's Elbow. Go through the gate at the end onto a track, which leads between walls to the moor. Look back as you follow this track for a good view of the grim, grey bulk of Dartmoor Prison dominating the village behind you. Go through another gate and keep on the same track, with a wall on your left, South Hessary Tor ahead of you and Hart Tor to the right, with the moors rolling away beyond.

When you reach South Hessary Tor, you will find superb views to both left and right, giving an excellent impression of the vastness of Dartmoor. Beyond the tor, keep following the line of the wall. You can see the Devonport Leat, which you will be meeting later in the walk, shimmering in the distance as it winds away to the left.

As the wall turns away to the left, go straight on, still with a lovely view of the moors stretching into the distance on the left. The PCWW (Plymouth City Water Works) marker stones act as excellent route guides. About 1.5km (1 mile) from South Hessary Tor you cross a well-defined track and another lovely view opens up to the right, with Burrator Reservoir and Sheeps Tor in the middle distance - you can see as far as Cornwall on a clear day. After another 400m ($^1/_4$ mile) or so you cross another track. Keep straight on.

About 500m beyond this second track, you will come to Siward's Cross, also known as Nun's Cross. This is the earliest recorded cross on the moor. It is named as a bondmark (boundary mark) of the Forest of Dartmoor in 1240, but is almost certainly much older, possibly dating back to the eleventh century, when one Siward, Earl of Northumberland, held two manors in this part of Devon. The name Siward (or Syward) can still just be made out inscribed on one side.

Turn left at the cross, over a wall, leaving the farm building of Nun's Cross Farm on your right. Go through a gap in the next wall and bear right towards a stream. A track runs down the hill, crossing Devonport Leat. This watercourse was built in the eighteenth century to take water from the West Dart and Cowsic rivers down to Devonport, now part of Plymouth - a distance of 43km (27 miles). This was quite a feat for that era, and as you can see as you cross it, it has stood the test of time.

After the leat, the track crosses the stream and then narrows to a path as it climbs the opposite bank, and finally peters out. Bear left parallel to the wall which runs in a straight line on your left, with extensive views beyond it. Follow the wall for about 1.5km (1 mile), passing a gully which comes down from the right. You will see a second gully on the right ahead of you; shortly before you reach it, turn left through a gateway in the wall. Childe's Tomb is clearly visible half left.

The 'tomb' consists of a nineteenth-century cross on a stone plinth, and is in fact built on the site of an ancient Bronze Age burial chamber (but not that of 'Childe' Ordulf who, as we have seen, was buried at Tavistock Abbey). It lies on the southern edge of the notorious Foxtor Mires, which have ensnared many an unwary traveller, and were the inspiration for the Great Grimpen Mire in Sir Arthur Conan Doyle's classic Sherlock Holmes mystery *The Hound of the Baskervilles*. Do not go straight on (north) from Childe's Tomb or you are likely to find yourself in the Mires. Instead turn left and follow the line of the wall. You will cross a rough and slightly marshy patch and then meet a faint but unmistakable path. Go right.

The path skirts Foxtor Mires, passing a cross along the way. It crosses a stream and then winds to the right, bringing you out at a gateway in a wall. Go through into the abandoned tin workings of Whiteworks and follow a track alongside a wall on the right, and then between two walls, to the end of a road. Turn right here (signposted 'public bridlepath') and follow a track to a gate into a field. Beyond the gate, the track curves right and then left. As it goes to the left, leave it to cross a stream and climb the low hill ahead. As you climb, the mast on North Hessary Tor comes into view on your left, and there is a good view of the empty moorland stretching away on your right.

At the top of the hill, cross a fence via a ladder stile and keep straight on, following the line of the fence on your right. You pass a small stone circle and cross a stream, and then you are faced with a lovely view of rolling moors ahead, with Bellever Tor straight in front of you. Keep heading towards Bellever Tor, and soon the great dome of Longaford Tor will appear half left, with Beardown Tors further round.

When you come to a fence, turn left and follow the rough track which runs parallel to it, heading straight towards the mast on North Hessary Tor. (This track was built by conscientious objectors who were detained in Dartmoor Prison during the First World War.)

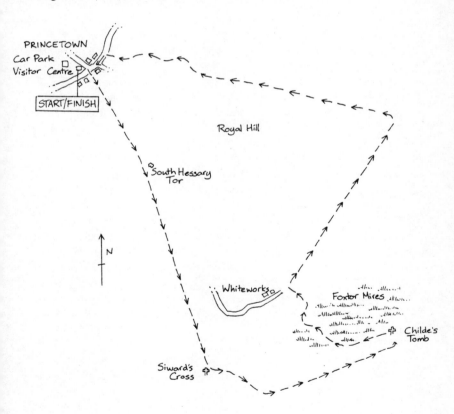

After about 1.5km (1 mile), you will pass a track going off to the left. Keep straight on, and after 500m (just over ¼ mile) the track you are on merges with one coming in from the left. Go straight on to the gate ahead, and through it into a lane. Just beyond the house on the right, turn right (signposted 'path'), go through another gate and follow a track which turns to the left and then to the right. At the junction, turn left (signposted to Princetown), cross the Devonport Leat again and go through another gate. There are more superb moorland views to the right and behind you.

Soon Princetown appears ahead of you, with the forbidding walls of the prison over on the right. Go through yet another gate onto a track, which winds between a fence and a wall to a road. Turn left and follow the road back to the village and the Visitor Centre on the right.

13. The Dancing Maidens

THE DANCERS

THE STORY

The Dancers, also known as Kiss-in-the-Ring, is a well-preserved stone circle on Stall Moor. The story connected with it is a simple one. The tweny-six stones that make up the circle are said to have been young maidens who loved to dance.

They were seen dancing up here one Sunday, and were turned to stone for their sin, although why they should come to such a remote spot just to dance one cannot imagine!

As with the story of the Nine Maidens (see Walk 3), it is possible that the story is connected with witchcraft, and that the maidens were turned to stone not for dancing on the Sabbath, but for disturbing a witches' sabbat or ritual. The circle, positioned as it is at the end of a long stone row, almost certainly had some ritual significance originally, although probably not one connected with witchcraft.

THE WALK

Start and finish: Shipley Bridge, between South Brent and the Avon Dam. Grid Ref. 681629

Parking: There is a large car park at Shipley Bridge.

Length: 14km (8³/₄ miles)

Approximate time: 3¹/₂ - 4 hours

Degree of difficulty: C

Route summary: If you have a penchant for vast expanses, enormous skies and a silence broken only by the singing of birds and the bleating of lambs, then this is definitely the walk for you - and there are some lovely views and several ancient and more recent features to give added interest. The route takes in few steep climbs, but the ground can be rough at times and there are a couple of river crossings to negotiate, so stout shoes or boots are recommended.

Take the path from the back of the car park, past the toilets. This joins the road up to the Avon Dam, which runs alongside the River Avon. It is a lovely stretch, with a mass of rhododendrons on the other side of the river. Just before the road forks, you will see a large stone on your left, with various names carved on it. This is the Hunters' Stone, which commemorates well-known members of the local hunt. At the beginning of the century, there were just four names: Treby, Trelawney and Bulteel on the sides and Carew on the top, but a number have been added more recently.

At the fork in the road, turn left and climb steeply among the bracken and gorse. At the gate to the treatment works, go right, up a sunken track alongside a wall. Where the wall turns left, go straight on up a well-worn track, the route of an old tramway which was used by the china clay works at Red Lake further north. There is a good view to the left and behind you as you follow this track.

It curves round to the right, following the contour of the hill, with the valley of the Bala Brook down to the left. It is here that one first becomes aware of the incredible stillness, a stillness which the occasional call of a bird or the bleating of a lamb only seems to accentuate.

You will see the strange shape of Eastern White Barrow, an ancient burial mound, on the horizon ahead of you. As you approach it, the track curves to the left. Follow it round. It becomes less distinct, but is still clear enough to follow as it skirts the marshy area that marks the head of Bala Brook on the left. Look back for a lovely view down the valley.

After a while, the rounded shapes of Stall Moor and Langcombe Hill appear in the distance ahead of you. Carry straight on towards them rather than following the sunken track which heads off to the right. Your route now takes you downhill, and you come to another, much clearer track, also a dismantled tramway leading to Red Lake. This is the route of the Two Moors Way, a long-distance path which goes from the southern edge of Dartmoor to the northern edge of Exmoor.

Cross this track and follow the gully down on the other side, keeping to the right. At the bottom is the River Erme, and on your right is a large stone enclosure. Go right, through the enclosure, to follow the river upstream to a much larger and better preserved enclosure. This is Erme Pound. Built on the site of an ancient settlement, it was used for centuries as a drift pound; any animals found on this part of the moor whose owners were not entitled to graze them here were brought to Erme Pound, and the owners had to pay a fee to reclaim them.

Go through Erme Pound down to the river and cross it - there are a number of stepping stones, and crossing is not difficult. Go up the other side and you will meet the remains of an old stone row. Many of the stones are overgrown and some are missing, but the line is unmistakable. You are now in the middle of the longest ancient stone row in Britain, stretching for some 3.5km (over 2 miles) from the Dancers in the south to a burial chamber on Green Hill in the north.

Turn left and follow the stones. There is nothing here to remind you of the modern world, just rolling hills, the vast, open sky and absolute peace - your imagination can run riot!

The stone row crosses a stream and passes a cairn on the right. After a little more than 1km (about ¾ mile) it ends in a stone circle. This is the Dancers, an impressive circle, some 16m (about 50ft) in diameter.

From the Dancers, go half left down to cross the river. It is fairly steep near the bottom, but quite manageable. There are several places where you can cross, and once across you should climb diagonally up the other side, heading downstream. Keep to the hillside rather than the valley, leaving the bracken-covered slopes to your right. There is no real path, just the odd sheep track, but the going is not too difficult.

You will see the outline of Sharp Tor on the horizon ahead of you, but you should aim to the left of it. You cross two streams and climb diagonally up the hill on the other side. At the top you will see Sharp Tor again, and there is a lovely view down the valley. Still keep Sharp Tor to your right, aiming for the track you can see running up to the saddle to the left of it.

When you join the track (the dismantled tramway you crossed higher up),

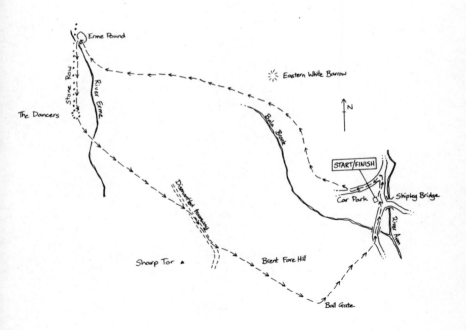

turn right. You can see for miles down the valley from here - a patchwork of fields and woodland. You will pass a small embankment on your left. About 100m beyond the embankment, shortly before the track curves to the right, cut up left. There is a narrow path you can follow, but if you miss it it doesn't matter - as long as you leave the track at about this point, you will not go wrong.

You cross a fairly wide track and another patchwork panorama opens up ahead. Cross an earth bank and you will see a rock-strewn hill up ahead. Keep this to your left. There is no real path, but the ground is quite easy. As you come round the hill, you will see a wall in the distance, with a track just visible stretching away from you on the other side. Aim for that.

When you reach the gate leading to the track, turn left and cut across to the corner of the wall. Soon a second wall comes in from the left, and the path runs between the two. When the left-hand wall turns away to the left, keep following the right-hand one down to a gate. Go through to a cool but rough path among some trees. It goes down to another gate leading onto a road. Turn left and follow the road as it curves right to cross a bridge, then left up a steep hill. At the top you can see Shipley Tor on the right and the car park below it. Cross a cattle grid and follow the road round to the right to return to the car park.

14. Tom White and the Pixies

LAUGHTER TOR

THE STORY

Pixies have a special place in the folklore of Dartmoor, and this tale demonstrates the love of fun and mischief for which they are renowned.

Tom White, a farmer from the Postbridge area (some versions of the tale actually specify Higher Cherrybrook), was courting a young girl at Huccaby, on the West Dart River near Hexworthy, and he would often walk across the moors to see her after his evening chores.

One night after visiting her, he set off home. He was just approaching Laughter Tor when he heard music and the sound of laughter and merrymaking. He peered round a rock to see what was happening, and there before him was a party of pixies having a dance.

He was so entranced that he stayed watching longer than he should have done, and one of the pixies saw him. He was immediately pulled into the ring and made to dance with them. At first it was fun, but he soon became tired. The pixies refused to let him leave, however, and he had to dance until dawn. Finally, he was allowed to make his way home, exhausted. He vowed that he would never go out on the moor at night again, which meant that his poor sweetheart never saw him again.

THE WALK

Start and finish: Higher Cherrybrook Bridge, on the B3212 between Two Bridges and Postbridge. Grid Ref. 634770

Parking: There is a car park on the right-hand side of the road just beyond the bridge as you approach from Two Bridges.

Length: 11.5km (7 miles)

Approximate time: 3-3$\frac{1}{2}$ hours

Degree of difficulty: B

Links with: Walk 17

Route summary: This is a fairly long but by no means difficult walk. It follows the ancient Lichway for a short distance through the cool greenery of Bellever Forest, then cuts across open moorland to Huccaby and brings you back via Laughter Tor and Bellever Tor with its spectacular panoramic views.

Turn left from the car park, through a gate marked 'Lichway and Bellever Tor'. There is a clear path leading up to Bellever Forest, with gorse and heather alongside. At the top, cross a stile to enter the forest. A broad track leads off ahead of you, with the dark and gloomy plantation on either side.

There is a lot of opposition to the presence of large plantations of conifers on Dartmoor - their geometric shape and dark green colour do not blend well with the moorland landscape, and they tend to inhibit rather than encourage the natural flora and fauna of the area. However, once one is in them, they are not unattractive places to walk through, and in summer they can provide a respite from the glare of the sun.

The track you are on is part of the Lichway or Lych Path, an ancient route across the moor. The name derives from the Old English for corpse, still preserved in the word 'lich-gate', the entrance gate to a church, where coffins were rested while the mourners waited for the clergyman. At one time everyone had to be buried in the churchyard of the parish in which they had lived. This created great problems for some inhabitants of Dartmoor, as Lydford Parish covers the whole of the old Dartmoor Forest, as far east as Bellever. This meant that the dead person's family had to carry their coffin all the way across Dartmoor to Lydford for burial, and the Lichway was the route they followed. This eastern section has not been used for that purpose since 1260, when Bishop Branscombe of Exeter allowed inhabitants of this area to use Widecombe Church instead, but its route can still be traced, with a few gaps, from Bellever Bridge almost all the way to Lydford.

The path crosses a well-made track and continues straight on, with a large felled area on the right and the plantation still on the left. This stretch is followed by a wide, open grassy area, which you cross, keeping to the line of stones, to re-enter the plantation on the other side. Almost immediately, you cross a track, following the signpost for the Lichway to Bellever, and a bit further on another one, again following the signpost for the Lichway to Bellever. The route along here is very clear, and is marked by posts with red rings round them.

Soon after crossing the last track, you come to the end of the plantation and the path goes to the right, following the edge of the trees. At the end there is a gate on the left, marked 'Lichway'. Go through it and down a track to another gate, beyond which is a tarred road. This leads you past some houses, then the Forestry Commission offices and a youth hostel on the left. At the junction just beyond the youth hostel, go straight on.

At the Forestry Commission sign just before Bellever Bridge, turn right down a track (signposted 'public bridlepath Laughter Hole Farm and county road B3357 at Huccaby Cottage'). This takes you back into Bellever Forest, to a large car park with toilets. Just beyond the car park is a lovely picnic spot alongside the East Dart River.

Where a sign points right for forest walks, go straight on to a gate marked 'bridlepath'. Go through and straight on up a track, with the river just visible through the trees on your left. At the fork in the track, where the trees on the left end, go straight on (signposted to Laughter Hole Farm). Follow the track along the edge of the plantation. There is a beautiful variety of wild flowers along here, and soon a good view opens up, with Corndon Tor and Yar Tor half left.

Leave the plantation via a gate and go down a track between walls. You pass some farm buildings on the right and then go through another gate. Go straight on up the track on the other side (signposted to the county road B3357 at Huccaby Cottage). At the top, go through yet another gate onto the open moorland.

Go half left (signposted to Huccaby Cottage). There is no clear path, but it is fairly easy to make your way through the heather and gorse. Try to keep to a fairly straight line half left from the gate, skirting round the edge of the dip on your left, but don't be too concerned about the exact route as you can very easily compensate for any divergence from it later on.

Once past the dip, you cross the remains of a wall and find a lovely panorama of moors and farms rolling away to Princetown and beyond on your right. Then, as you come over the brow of the hill, you will see a wall ahead of you and a plantation on the left. Aim for the corner of the plantation and go through a gate in the wall.

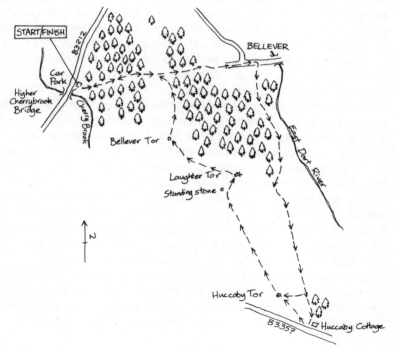

If you want to go to the very end of Tom White's route, you should follow the wall which runs alongside the plantation to the road at the bottom. Huccaby Cottage is just over the wall on the left, and Huccaby Farm across the road. It is not certain which was the home of Tom's sweetheart, but it was probably the farm. Neither, of course, is accessible to the public. At the road, turn sharp right, almost back on yourself, and climb to the pile of rocks which is Huccaby Tor.

You can avoid going all the way down to the road just to come up again by cutting straight across to Huccaby Tor from the gate. From Huccaby Tor, you can see across to Yar Tor and Sharp Tor to the east, to Combestone Tor, Holne Moor and Down Ridge across a patchwork of fields to the south and up the valley of the West Dart to the west.

From Huccaby Tor, head away from the road, to cross back over the wall by a stile. You will see Laughter Tor and Bellever Tor ahead, and a whole range of other tors stretching north from Princetown on the left. The path is very clear on the other side of the wall, and heads in an almost straight line through the heather and gorse towards Laughter Tor.

As you approach Laughter Tor, an extensive view opens up to your right, with Haytor on the horizon. You cross a wall to a large standing stone. There are stone rows running away from it over to the right, which indicates that it had some significance - probably religious - in prehistoric times. Bear right to climb gently up to Laughter Tor. On the way, you will pass the remains of a rectangular structure on your right. This is an old pound, which, according to William Crossing, in his *Guide to Dartmoor*, was used as a 'sheep measure'. 'Its capacity being known, when it was filled with these animals there was no need of counting them to ascertain their number!' It seems a rather haphazard way of counting sheep, but that is what Crossing was told!

The views from Laughter Tor are beautiful, and range through 360 degrees, stretching for miles in every direction. It is also quite easy to imagine the pixies dancing on the grassy areas at the top or in the surrounding area. From the top, turn left and make your way down through the heather and gorse to the corner of a wall running along the edge of the plantation on your right. Follow the wall to a gate at the end and turn right towards Bellever Tor.

You can go round to the right of Bellever Tor, following the edge of the plantation, but if you have the energy, it is worth climbing it. The views from the top are quite glorious - similar to those from Laughter Tor, but much better because you are higher. If you do climb the tor, then you should take the broad path which leads down on the other side towards the plantation again.

Cross the wall at the bottom of the hill, and go up the right-hand side of the broad swathe of open ground. When a track crosses your path, turn left. Cross the open ground into the plantation. You are now back on the Lichway, and can follow it straight through the plantation, through two gates and back to the car park.

15. The Faithless Wives of Chagford

THE TOLMEN

THE STORY

This is a fascinating legend, and one whose origins are probably buried in Dartmoor's distant past. Yet it is not very well known; the only written reference I have come across is in Ruth St Leger Gordon's *The Witchcraft and Folklore of Dartmoor*.

A long time ago in Chagford, 'faithless wives and fickle maidens' were made to atone for their sins by a long, arduous - and sometimes fatal - ritual in the wilds of Dartmoor. They had to run three times round Scorhill Circle, on Gidleigh Common, and were then chased down to the banks of the North Teign River where they were made to pass through the Tolmen, a large rock with a hole through it.

From there they had to make their way to Grey Wethers, two stone circles on the slopes of Sittaford Tor, where each woman knelt before one of the stones and prayed for forgiveness. If nothing happened, she could go home, absolved. But if her sins were too great, then the stone before which she was kneeling would fall over and crush her. 'And that,' said Mrs St Leger Gordon's informant, 'is why so many of the stones was lying flat before they was set up again.'

It is said that the women were required to wash in Cranmere Pool before going to Scorhill Circle, but that appears to be a later addition to the story, inserted after the pool became a popular pilgrimage place for walkers. Cranmere Pool is a very long way from Chagford, and if washing were necessary as part of the ritual, there are many places closer to the rest of the route where it could have been done.

THE WALK

Start and finish: Chagford. Grid Ref. 702875
Parking: There is a large free car park at the end of the village, past the church.
Length: 21km (13 miles)
Approximate time: 5-6 hours
Degree of difficulty: C
Route summary: Although this is a long walk, it is not too difficult. There is one long hill towards the beginning and a rough stretch in the middle, but the rest is relatively easy going. It takes you along the route followed by the unfortunate 'faithless wives', down country lanes, across open moor and past an attractive reservoir. There are one or two excellent views, some magnificent expanses of moorland and some delightful woodland. And when you get back, there is a choice of four pubs at which to quench your thirst - what more could you ask?

Chagford is an ancient stannary town, where the miners of Dartmoor used to bring their tin to be assessed and weighed. It is a very attractive village, with its cluster of shops and pubs around the Square.

From the car park go past the church and down High Street. As you go, you will pass the attractive stone porch of the Three Crowns Hotel on your left. It was in this porch that the poet and ardent royalist Sidney Godolphin died, after being shot in battle during the Civil War.

Carry straight on down High Street, through the village, and at the junction by the Moorland Hotel go straight on down Mill Street (signposted to Gidleigh and Throwleigh). This takes you out of the village and down a hill. At the crossroads at the bottom, go right (signposted to Gidleigh and Throwleigh again), and cross the pretty old packhorse bridge.

On the other side, look out for a stile on the left and a footpath sign pointing to Murchington. Cross the stile and follow the path into some pretty woodland. There is a short climb, and then the path forks. Go right, away from the river. Bear left at the path sign to cross a stream and a stile into a field.

Go straight up the left-hand side of the field. It is a steep climb, but mercifully short, and ends at a stile into a lane. Cross the stile and turn left. At the junction, go straight on (signposted to Gidleigh). You pass some lovely old stone farms and cottages, and climb again. Go straight on at the next junction (signposted to Gidleigh again), and as you come over the hill, you will be met by a view of farms and woods, with the moors in the distance.

The road descends again and curves to the right. There are masses of hedgerow flowers along here. At the bottom the lane winds through woodland, then curves left to cross a stream and starts a long climb on the other side.

At the next junction, go straight on (signposted to Berrydown and Scorhill). The lane curves right round some houses and then left again. Where it turns sharply to the right, go straight on, up another lane marked with a 'No through road' sign. At the end, go through a gate onto the open moor.

Keep to the left-hand wall, and at the corner look back for a superb panorama of woods and farms. Where the wall goes away to the left, follow the path that leads straight on up to the wide open spaces of Gidleigh Common. This magnificent expanse of empty moorland stretches away before you, punctuated only by the rather intrusive green of the odd plantation in the distance.

Soon you will see a stone circle down in the valley half right. This is Scorhill Circle, one of the finest on Dartmoor, well preserved and with some sizeable stones - the biggest is about 2.5m (8ft) tall. If you take a break here, especially on a summer day, one of the first things you will notice is the incredible silence all around. You might hear the occasional lark, or a sheep bleating in the distance, but otherwise nothing. Surrounded by the empty moorland, cocooned in the absolute stillness, it is very easy to understand why our distant ancestors found this a very special place and built a stone circle here - whatever its actual purpose might have been.

Turn left from Scorhill Circle, aiming for the line of trees across the valley. Cross a small stream and clamber over some rocks to reach the river bank.

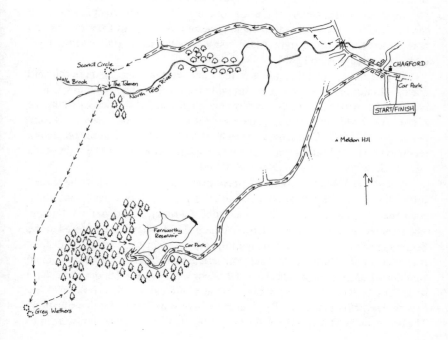

Immediately opposite the wall which runs down alongside the trees on the other side, you will find the Tolmen - an enormous boulder with a hole right through it. The hole was made quite naturally, at a time when the river was deeper, by the action of small pebbles gradually wearing down the rock over hundreds of years as they were swirled around by the current. Apart from its association with the story of the 'faithless wives', the Tolmen was also said to have healing properties. Anyone who passed through the hole was believed to be cured of rheumatism. If you are tempted to try it yourself, however, just consider how you are going to get back up to the bank. And if the river is in spate, don't try it at all, or you could end up being washed downstream.

Turn right to follow the Walla Brook, which runs into the North Teign, upstream for a short distance. Cross it via a small clapper bridge, then turn left and go downstream a little way to a second clapper bridge across the North Teign on the right, at a place called Teign-e-ver. This rather strange name (which some say should be spelt simply 'Teignever') unfortunately has no exotic origin, but is believed to be simply a corruption of 'Teignaford', 'the ford over the Teign'.

From Teign-e-ver, go half right, bearing away from the wall towards the right-hand side of the plantation you can see on the skyline. There is no path, and the ground is rather rough and fairly marshy. Pick your way through or round the marshy parts, which may mean diverging somewhat from your direct line. But as long as you aim generally to the right of the plantation, the exact line does not matter. You will soon see a wall running across the ridge in front of you and across the valley to your right. Make you way round to the right of this ridge, crossing a stream as you go.

As you come round the corner of the ridge, you will see a gate in the wall ahead. Go through it and continue straight up the valley. The plantation is now half left. Keep to the left of the marshy area and the small hill ahead, passing the remains of an old settlement as you do so. There are extensive views back from here across Gidleigh Common. Bear right to follow the wall and the plantation down to cross a stile at the end. Follow the path that runs just to the right of the wall, with Sittaford Tor straight ahead of you.

Where the plantation boundary veers to the left, you cross a wall. Do not follow the line of the plantation here, but go straight on. It is a clear path, which soon bears right to a gate in the wall ahead. Go through it, and you will find the two impressive stone circles of Grey Wethers ahead. They were restored at the beginning of this century, and many of the fallen stones were set upright again. It is interesting to visit any ancient stone circle and speculate about its original significance and the ideas and beliefs of the people who built it. I find it particularly so at Grey Wethers, however, because of the additional questions it raises: Why two circles? Why is one smaller than the other? Why this particular situation? The name, incidentally, is derived simply from the stones' supposed likeness to sheep from a distance - a wether being a castrated ram. The stones of these circles are said to get up and walk around at sunrise.

Turn left at Grey Wethers and follow the wall towards the plantation. Go through the gate straight ahead at the end. There is a lovely view stretching out ahead of you over Fernworthy Reservoir and farmland for miles into the distance. Follow the track as it goes left into the plantation. Although this is the largest plantation on Dartmoor, it does not seem quite as obtrusive as many of the others, perhaps because the reservoir softens its lines somewhat. It does stand out in the distance like the proverbial sore thumb, but once in it, it is not unpleasant to walk through.

At the junction in the track, go right. As the trees open up on the right, you will see the view across the reservoir to the farmland beyond again. At the next junction go right again. The track begins to descend towards the reservoir and you cross another, more minor, track. At the next junction bear right and the reservoir comes into view through the trees. Go through a gate and turn right onto a road.

Follow the road round the end of the reservoir. You pass through a variety of woodland as you go - conifers of course, but interspersed with broadleaved trees - and there are a number of places where you can leave the road and go down to pretty picnic sites by the water. Keep following the road and you will pass the main car park, with toilets and a picnic site, on the left. You leave the plantation soon afterwards, crossing a cattle grid, and come to open moorland. As you follow the road, there is a delightful variety of scenery all around - open moorland behind you, Thornworthy Tor on the left, and a magnificent panorama of farms and woods ahead and to the right, with Meldon Hill half right.

The road dips down to a cattle grid and you leave the moors as it runs between hedges to a junction. Go straight on (signposted to Chagford). After about 1.25km (³/₄ mile), you will find Meldon Hill looming above you on the right, with an extensive patchwork of fields stretching away on the left. You join another road and carry straight on (signposted to Chagford). After about 1km (¹/₂ mile) it curves to the right and descends before climbing steeply into the village. Follow it as it curves right at the top into High Street and go back past the church to the car park.

16. Old Dewer and the Dewerstone

THE DEWERSTONE

THE STORY

The Dewerstone is a huge rock, some 100m (325ft) high, which rises above the River Plym near Shaugh Bridge. It is here that the victims of the Devil (known on the moor as Old Dewer) meet their fate.

Dewer sallies forth from Wistman's Wood, near Two Bridges, at night, riding his headless black horse and acompanied by his pack of black Wisht Hounds. But his is no ordinary hunt - he is after human, not animal, prey. In some versions of the story, he drives his victims across the moors to the Dewerstone, in others he lures curious onlookers there. Once there, however, their fate is the same: they fall from the enormous rock to their death in the gorge below, to the eerie accompaniment of hollow laughter, baying, thunder-claps and vivid blue flames. It is also said that anyone who sees them will die within the year.

Legend tells of a man who heard the baying of the hounds when he was out one night, accompanied by terrified screams. He approached the top of the cliff and peered over. There, in the snow below, he saw a pack of enormous hounds devouring a human body. He ran away in terror, but the following morning he returned with some friends. Imprinted in the snow at the top of the rock they found the shapes of a human foot and a cloven hoof, but there was no sign of any human remains down below - just some bloodstains and a torn cloak.

In another version of the story Dewer has a particular penchant for the souls of unbaptised babies, and the tale is told of a man wandering home from the pub late one night and meeting the hunt on its way back to Wistman's Wood. Full of Dutch courage, the man called out to Dewer and asked if he had had good hunting. 'Yes,' came the reply. 'And since you ask, here's something for you.' And he threw down a sack. The man hurried home and opened the sack, only to find the remains of his baby daughter inside.

THE WALK

Start and finish: Shaugh Bridge. Grid Ref. 532637

Parking: There are two car parks at the bridge, one on either side. It is best to use the one on the Shaugh Prior side, but if that is full (which it might be, as this is a very popular picnic area), use the one on the other side and walk across the bridge to start the walk. Do not try to start the walk from the second car park, as you could find yourself following the River Meavy rather than the Plym - the two come together at Shaugh Bridge.

Length: 5.5km (3½ miles)

Approximate time: 1½ hours

Degree of difficulty: A

Route summary: Apart from a steep climb near the beginning, this is an easy route which takes you through beautiful National Trust woodland along the banks of the River Plym and up to the top of the Dewerstone, from which the views are superb. You then walk across open moorland to Cadover Bridge and come back through the woods again.

The woods around Shaugh Bridge are stunningly beautiful and very popular with families and picnickers. On leaving the car park, you head straight into them. Bear left to cross a wooden footbridge and go through a gate on the other side. Bear right after the gate onto a broad path paved with granite. The river is lovely along here, rushing and cascading over the rocks, and it is not surprising that the area is so popular. The path climbs away from the river, however, running vaguely parallel to it.

Soon you will see a path leading off to the right. This leads to the Dewerstone Rocks, a cluster of rocks around the Dewerstone, and from there via some steps to the foot ot the Dewerstone itself. This is a very popular area for rock climbing, and there are some interesting climbs. It is probably not a worthwhile detour for the walker, however, since you will almost certainly have to retrace your steps along the same path to continue the walk. You can climb up out of the valley via a gully on the other side of the rock, but it is a difficult scramble, and the route is not recommended for any but the fittest and best equipped of walkers.

The main path climbs and winds through a lovely broadleaved woodland, with the river still audible below. It is easy to follow, as it is the most obvious path for most of the way. It is only towards the top that you may become confused. Here you will find a path going straight on and another winding sharp right. Take the latter, turning almost back on yourself. The paving ends and soon you will see the top of the Dewerstone on your right.

The path goes left, climbing steeply away from the river and the Dewerstone. After a short climb you leave the woods, cross a wall and climb up to the rocks ahead of you. This is the site of an Iron Age hill fort, and a magnificent place it is. There are views across Plymouth to Cornwall to the west, to the sea to the south and over rich, green farmland to the moors to the north.

You are now on open moorland. Turn right and follow the path which runs through the bracken towards the edge of the woods and a group of rocks. Pass the rocks and go on until you reach a wall. Turn left and follow the wall round. As you go, you will see on your right the china clay works scarring the landscape on the other side of the river.

Keep following the wall as it curves round to the right and soon, beyond the china clay works, a vast stretch of moorland comes into view, disappearing into the distance. The wall winds in and out, and after about 1km (½ mile) you will come to a cross. As you pass it, you will notice that it has been repaired - the cross itself has been 'grafted' onto a new shaft.

Go down to the road at Cadoyer Bridge, It gets its name from the Celtic *cad*, meaning 'battle', which would suggest that this was the site of some kind of skirmish in ancient times. It is said that the cries of the warriors and the clash of their weapons can still be heard from time to time. Cross the bridge and turn right to go through the car park. Cross a stile to enter the woods, and after a short distance cross another stile. The path follows a disused - and now broken - pipeline, down which the china clay was pumped, suspended in water, to a drying plant lower down the Plym Valley. There is a grassy bank on your left and the river cascades away down on your right.

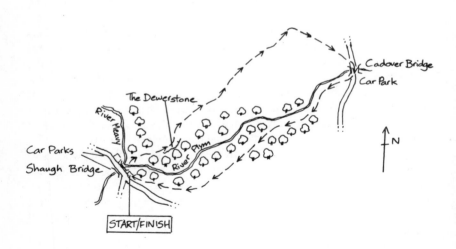

After a while the path drops down a level via a ladder and you cross a wooden footbridge. The whole wood seems to have a green glow along here, as the rocks and tree-trunks are covered in moss and lush grass carpets the slope down to the river.

Cross a stile onto a bracken-covered hillside. You are now some way above the river, and a good view opens up ahead, across Plymouth to Cornwall. You can also see the Dewerstone and its associated rocks across the valley on your right. Still following the old pipeline, the path re-enters the woods and starts to descend.

You soon come to a gate onto a track. Do not go through it, but follow the path round to the right and alongside the track. It comes out into an open patch. Follow the 'path' signs, which will very soon direct you back into the woods. The path goes downhill to a stile. Cross it and carry on down to the road at the end. Turn right and follow the path which runs parallel to the road. At the fork, go left down some steps to the car park.

17. The Phantom Pigs of Merripit Hill

POSTBRIDGE

THE STORY

This strange and rather pathetic little tale is one of the most enduring of Dartmoor stories, but where it has sprung from remains a mystery. It is quite unlike any of the other legends of the moor.

On dull, misty days, it is said, a sow and her litter of hungry piglets make their way from Merripit Hill, just north-east of Postbridge, to Cator, on the way to Widecombe. Having heard that there is a dead pony there and hoping for a share in the carcass, they can be seen wandering along squeaking, 'Dead 'oss. Dead 'oss.'

When they get there, however, they find that there is nothing left of the pony but skin and bones, so they have to turn around and trudge sadly back to Merripit, still hungry, muttering mournfully, 'Skin 'n' bones. Skin 'n' bones.' As they go, they become thinner and thinner until they finally dissolve into the mist - only to emerge again on another foggy day.

THE WALK

Start and finish: Postbridge. Grid Ref. 646789
Parking: There is a large car park at Postbridge.
Length: 12km (7¹/₂ miles)
Approximate time: 3 hours
Degree of difficulty: B
Links with: Walks 7 and 14
Route summary: Although this is a fairly long walk, it is very easy, with no climbing to speak of and very little rough ground. It takes you from the foot of

72

Merripit Hill down across Cator Common to Cator and back via Bellever Plantation and along the East Dart River. There are lovely views and some gorgeous stretches of open moorland, and on the latter part of the route you are seldom far from the sight or sound of tumbling streams.

On leaving the car park, turn left along the road to go through the hamlet of Postbridge. Cross the bridge, noticing the ancient clapper bridge, one of the most photographed structures on Dartmoor, on your right as you do so. You pass the East Dart Hotel on your right, and then the village hall and the pretty little church. About 1.25km (³/₄ mile) from the car park, you cross a cattle grid and turn right (signposted to Widecombe). The rather insignificant-looking hill half left from the cattle grid is Merripit Hill, home of the phantom pigs. You can climb it if you wish - a track leads up about 500m beyond the cattle grid - but it is hardly worth the detour.

Follow the Widecombe road past farms on the right, with open moorland on the left - a purple mass of heather in the summer, dotted with the bright yellow of gorse. There are extensive views to the right and behind you, with Yar Tor on the horizon half right and Bellever Plantation on the right.

A wall and a fence come in from the left, closing off the open moorland on that side. As you walk along between the two fences, a new view opens up ahead, and Soussons Plantation comes into sight half left. The road winds gently downhill, past Runnage Farm on the left. Cross Runnage Bridge, and Soussons Plantation will be immediately on your left, with heather-covered moorland on the right.

About 500m beyond the bridge, there is a small track going off to the right. Follow this and cross a raised bank about 10m from the road, passing a boundary stone marked CB (which stands for Cator bounds) as you go. It will take you to a gate in a fence. If you happen to miss the track (and it is not very obvious from the road), don't worry. Simply make your way through the heather and gorse to the fence and walk along it until you come to the gate.

Go through the gate onto Cator Common. The track is very clear as it crosses the common, with good views to left and right, taking in a mixture of farms, moorland and woods. It leads to a row of trees. Turn right to follow the trees to a gate onto a road. Turn left and follow the road down through the trees. There is another good view over the moorland to the right, and Yar Tor reappears half right. Go through a gateway and then between two walls, passing the turning to Cator Court, to another gateway leading to the open moors.

Follow the track leading off to the right just beyond the gateway, and after a few metres branch off to the left, following the footpath sign which points to Sherril and Dartmeet. It is a broad path running among the gorse and heather which form a variegated carpet of yellow and purple in the summer. This is a particularly beautiful stretch, with the smooth, treeless curves of the hills up ahead, the sky forming an enormous vault above, and silence all around.

As you approach the wall ahead, the path forks. Go left, aiming for the finger post on the horizon at the corner of the wall. The path runs alongside the wall for a short way, and then veers off to the left. Yar Tor is now straight ahead. To the left there is still a mixture of heather and gorse, but on the right they are replaced by bracken. The path descends to Sherwell Farm. Keep the buildings on your left and go down to meet a road.

Turn right and follow the road. Ignore the footpath sign pointing off to the left just beyond the farm buildings and keep to the road as it winds down, with a little stream running along beside it. Cross a stream at the bottom and go on to the gate leading to Babeny Farm. A few metres beyond the gate, turn right, following the bridlepath sign, and then left past the farm buildings, following the blue arrows. There is a short climb up a track, which runs alongside a wall at the top, curving to the right and then to the left.

Go through the gate at the end and straight on, as the track continues to follow the line of the wall on the left, but a few metres above it. The track soon narrows to a path, but it is still quite clear. Laughter Hole House is straight ahead of you, with Bellever Plantation on the horizon behind it. The path descends quite steeply to a gate and some stepping stones across the East Dart River (signposted to forest paths, Bellever and Postbridge).

On the other side of the river, go left through another gate and then bear right. Ignore the path which leads off to the left across a ladder stile and carry straight on (signposted to Laughter Hole Farm). Cross a small wooden footbridge and climb to a gate. Go through and keep climbing (signposted to Bellever). You are now on a track which takes you past an area of felled conifers.

At the top, turn right through a gateway and follow the track among newly planted trees until it joins another track. Go right (signposted to Bellever again) and through the gate ahead. You pass some farm buildings on the left and eventually come to another gate. Beyond this gate go straight on along the edge of the trees rather than left into the plantation.

After a few hundred metres, the trees close in on both sides, and a little further on, as the track goes off to the left, you should go straight on through a gate (signposted 'path'). There is a picnic area on the left, but if you want to stop there is a much nicer area down to the right on the riverbank. Just beyond the picnic area, you pass some toilets and then a car park, and finally emerge from the plantation onto a road.

Cross the road and bear left to follow a wall. Go through a gate marked 'bridleway' and follow the path alongside the road. At the end of the hedge on the right, bear right to climb up onto some open ground. At the top, the high moors stretch away into the distance ahead. Cross a track to a small plantation on the right and the wall beyond. You may have to pick your way across a boggy patch in wet weather, or you can avoid it altogether by skirting round to the left.

Follow the wall and as you approach Postbridge the path will take you steeply down to a gate in a fence near the river. Beyond the gate it passes the clapper bridge (another very pleasant place for a picnic) and emerges onto the road via another gate. Turn left to go back to the car park.

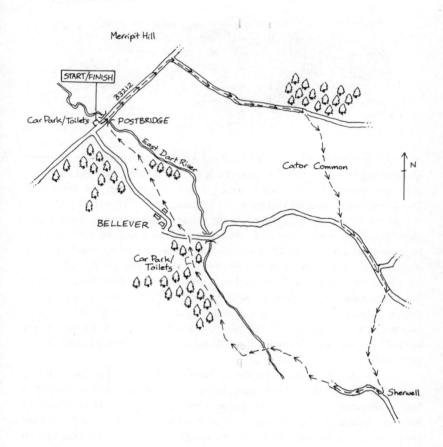

18. The Legends of Crazywell Pool

CRAZYWELL POOL

THE STORIES

Considering that Crazywell Pool is no more than an old mine working which has filled with water, it is surprising how many legends it has generated. It was said, for example, that when the bellropes of Walkhampton Church were tied together and lowered into it, they did not reach the bottom, whereas in fact it is no more than 4.5m (15ft) deep. It was also said that the level rose and fell with the tide at Plymouth - another fallacy, since it has no connection with the sea, although the level does fluctuate quite considerably at times of heavy rain or drought.

There was a local superstition that at dusk and at dawn a voice could be heard emanating from the pool, calling the name of the next person to die in the parish; because of this, the locals tended to give the area a wide berth in case they heard their own name. Another story (or another version of the same story) has it that if you look into the water on Midsummer Eve, you will see the face of the next person to die.

The pool is said to be frequented by the Witch of Sheeps Tor, and there is a story that Piers Gaveston, a one-time favourite of Edward II who was banished from court, came here to consult her about his future. She told him that 'his humbled head shall soon be high', which he took as a good omen. In fact her words had a double meaning: he was beheaded and his head displayed high on the walls of Warwick Castle!

Sadly, this interesting story appears to be the figment of one man's imagination; it derives from a poem by the Revd John Johns. Gaveston did have connections with Dartmoor (he was Warden) and local tradition has it that he sought refuge on the moor when he was banished. But there is nothing except the poem to connect him with Crazywell Pool.

THE WALK

Start and finish: The dam wall at Burrator Reservoir. Grid Ref. 550680

Parking: There is parking alongside the road at the dam wall. Alternatively, there is a large parking area on the left-hand side of the road leading to the reservoir, about 300m before the dam wall.

Length: 10km (6¼ miles)

Approximate time: 2½ hours

Degree of difficulty: B

Route summary: Burrator is one of the most attractive of Dartmoor's reservoirs, and the woods and plantations that surround it are extremely pleasant to walk through - not the tightly packed, single-species conifer stands that one sees elsewhere, but a mixture of conifers and broadleaved trees, well spaced and with delightful glades and clearings. This route takes you up one side of the reservoir (with the opportunity to climb to a superb viewpoint along the way), out onto the open moors to Crazywell Pool, and back down the other side. It is all easy going, along roads and forest tracks, with just one short, 500m stretch across the open moor.

Follow the road past the dam wall, with the reservoir on your right, and Sheeps Tor on the skyline beyond. After about 250m, there is a beautiful stream cascading down on the left and under the road into the reservoir. The rhododendrons along here are splendid in the spring.

Where the road forks, go right (signposted to Norsworthy Bridge). You go in and out of a variety of woodland - sometimes conifers, sometimes broadleaved trees, sometimes a mixture of the two. The reservoir is visible from time to time on the right, with Sheeps Tor still dominating the horizon behind it and Down Tor half right.

You cross the Devonport Leat, a remarkable feat of eighteenth-century engineering. It was built to carry water from the West Dart and Cowsic Rivers to Devonport, now part of Plymouth, a distance of 43km (27 miles). It now empties into Burrator Reservoir. Leather Tor looms up ahead and then the trees close in again.

Soon you come to an open space on your left, with Leather Tor now half left. Make your way across this space, through the gorse and bracken, towards the tor. Cross the road to the car pull-in on the other side, crossing Devonport Leat again. You will see a cross on the right, consisting of the original cross-pieces set on a modern shaft. This was one of a series of crosses which marked an ancient monastic route across the moor. You will be following the route itself all the way from here to Crazywell Pool.

Follow the track which runs off to your right from the pull-in, parallel to the road and along the edge of the trees. Alternatively, if you are feeling energetic, you can go straight on to climb up to Leather Tor. It is a fairly steep climb, and there is some scrambling over rocks, but the views from up there are superb. If you are really energetic, you can climb the tor itself for an even more spectacular panorama. If you do climb up to Leather Tor, then I would suggest that you return the same way; although it is possible to come down on the eastern side and make your way back to the track that way, it is a very difficult route, involving a lot of scrambling and some very thick bracken.

From the pull-in, follow the main track, ignoring any side branches. It crosses the leat, and after about 500m enters the plantation through a gateway. (If you find yourself entering the plantation via a stile and following the line of the leat, it means you have forked left instead of keeping to the main track.)

This is a very pleasant stretch of woodland, comprising a mixture of conifers and a variety of broadleaved trees, well spaced so that there is enough light and room for other plants to grow beneath the canopy. The track winds down and along the valley floor. You can hear the River Meavy off to the right and soon you curve to the right and cross it via Leather Tor Bridge, a clapper bridge (though probably not a very old one) which has had parapets added to it.

Just after the bridge, go left, and at the next fork, go right, up the hill. A straight stretch follows, then a couple of bends. As the track nears the edge of the plantation and curves to the right for the second time, fork left up another track. This leads up to a gate and a stile and back among the trees. Cross the stile and go almost dead straight through the trees to another gate and another stile, leading out onto the open moor.

On the other side, instead of following the remains of the track as it curves to the left, bear slightly right to head directly away at right angles to the edge of the plantation. As you come over the rise, a depression will come into view ahead of you, with a cross about 100m beyond it. This is Crazywell Pool, and it so well hidden that you will probably not realise that it *is* a pool until you reach it. Since it is only about 400m (^{1}/$_4$ mile) from the edge of the plantation, however, you are unlikely to miss it. The cross is another of the series marking the old monastic way, but this is where you leave that route.

From Crazywell Pool, our way lies due south (to the right). You will find a gully leading off from the pool in that direction. Follow it down to a track. Turn right and follow the track to a gateway, with Newleycombe Lake flowing down on your left and Down Tor beyond. About 500m (a little over ^{1}/$_4$ mile) beyond the gateway the track forks. Go straight on. The reservoir is now straight ahead, with Leather Tor half right and Sheeps Tor half left.

The track winds steadily downhill through open country, until you begin to hear the sound of Newleycombe Lake on your left and then descend to the road at Norsworthy Bridge. Go left. This is a lovely wooded area, with the sound of the river never far away. You will soon find yourself in open country again, however, and then the road crosses a stream and curves to the right. The forest stretches down to the reservoir on your right and Sheeps Tor looms over you on the left. After a while the trees close in on the left and the reservoir becomes visible through the trees just down to the right.

The road follows the line of the reservoir bank closely along here, with just a narrow belt of trees alongside it on that side and mixed woodland on the left. It meanders gently along, but some 2km (1¼ miles) from Norsworthy Bridge it takes a sharp turn to the left, away from the reservoir and into a tunnel of trees. Instead of following it round, you should go straight on across a stile and onto a track. After a few hundred metres, this track curves to the right along the top of the dam wall. There is a good view up the reservoir to Peek Hill, Sharpitor and Leather Tor.

At the end of the wall you can cross the stile ahead onto the road again, or follow the grassy path which leads into the trees, and so avoid some of the road walking. It is a pretty path, sheltered from the road by large rhododendron bushes and close to the edge of the reservoir. After a while you come to a stile on the left, which leads onto the road. Cross it and turn right. Do not try to follow the path any further, even though it looks as though you can - you will only come to a blank wall. Follow the road across a second dam wall back to your car.

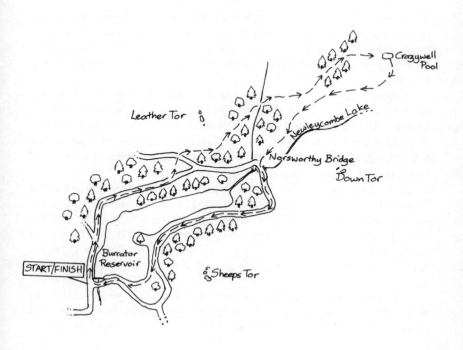

19. The Ghost of George Stephens

STEPHENS' GRAVE

THE STORY

George Stephens was a young man from Peter Tavy who committed suicide in October 1762. Apart from these bare details, there is very little definite information about him - indeed, some versions of his story even give his name as John, not George.

It appears, however, that he took his life because he was crossed in love. Some say that his sweetheart was unfaithful to him, others that she spurned his advances, and yet others that it was her parents who rejected him as unsuitable. One tradition has it that he took took his life by eating a poisoned apple, having first killed the girl by giving it to her; another says that he ate deadly nightshade. Most versions, however, simply say that he took poison.

At that time, suicides were refused Christian burial, and were usually interred far from the village and at a crossroads, in order to confuse their spirits and prevent them from returning to haunt the living. That is why Stephens' Grave is out on the open moor, and at a point where two paths cross. It is said that at the precise moment he was buried, some washing hanging out to dry at Higher Godsworthy Farm across the valley was whisked up into the air and never seen again.

His ghost is said to haunt the spot to this day, dressed in a grey shroud. It can be seen at night, sometimes sitting on the stone that marks the grave, sometimes darting about as if trying to find the way home.

THE WALK

Start and finish: Peter Tavy. Grid Ref. 514776
Parking: Alongside the road in the village. Please park with due consideration for other road users.
Length: 6km (3 ³/₄ miles)
Approximate time: 1¹/₂ hours
Degree of difficulty: A
Route summary: We follow the direct route from Peter Tavy out to Stephens' Grave, and return past Higher Godsworthy, where the washing is said to have disappeared at the time of the burial. It is a short and generally fairly easy walk, along well-defined paths, with just one or two short climbs. There is a superb view across west Devon and into Cornwall for much of the way.

At the road junction in the centre of Peter Tavy, go right, keeping the house called Jasmine Cottage on your left. Take the track which leads off to the left just beyond Jasmine Cottage. A few yards up it you will find a public bridlepath sign pointing to the Combe, but it is unfortunately not visible from the road. You pass the Methodist Church on the right and enter a short stretch of woodland, with the Colly Brook on the left.

At the end you come out onto a lane. Go left and cross the brook, following the lane up the hill past a row of cottages on the left. When the lane ends, follow the path which leads straight on into some trees. After a short distance, you go through a gate and come to a junction in the path. Do not go straight on down to the stream or sharp left through another gate, but turn half left, following the sign to the road near Lower Godsworthy.

At first this path runs roughly parallel to the Colly Brook through some bracken, but then it climbs to the left, up to a wall with a post marked with yellow on the top. There is a good view back the way you've come from here. Cross the wall, and then cross the field on the other side to a gate. Go through it and follow the path through the bracken up to a road.

Cross the road and follow the line of the wall on your right to a track. Turn right. A line of tors - White Tor, Roos Tor and Great Staple Tor - appears on the horizon ahead of you. There is a moderate climb and at the top the track curves to the right between two walls. Soon the walls veer away and you find yourself out on the open moor. White Tor is now half left, with the remains of a prehistoric settlement on the slope below.

Where the wall on your left turns away from the track, you will find Stephens' Grave on your right. It is marked by a simple black stone on a triangular plinth inscribed with the letter 'S'. This is a good place to take a break and appreciate the stillness of the moor and the magnificent view back across the fields. You can see Brent Tor in the distance with the church of St Michael perched on the very top.

Turn right at the grave, onto a broad path across the moor, with Roos Tor and Great Staple Tor ahead. Go down to the left-hand corner of the wall in front of you, and follow it round. Where it meets another wall coming in from the left, cross a stream and go through a gate marked 'bridlepath'. (If you come to a gate marked 'Wedlake', then you are too far to the right. You need to follow the wall to the left and go round the next corner to reach the right gate.)

Go through the gate and turn half right to cross a field to another gate. Go half right again, skirting a gully, to the corner of a wall. Follow the wall round to the right, and where it veers right again, go straight on. Higher Godsworthy is down on your right, and the view across to Brent Tor opens up again.

Soon you will join a road alongside a wall. Follow it for a short distance and just before the left-hand bend, turn right through a gate (signposted to Peter Tavy via the Combe). Follow the right-hand boundary of the field on the other side, and Brent Tor appears in the distance again. At the fork in the path, go right, through the gorse, to a gate in the far corner of the wall. This leads to a path between two walls, which soon opens up again at the jumble of rocks and outcrops that is Great Combe Tor. This is another good place to pause and admire the 180 degree panorama spread out before you.

Follow the path alongside the wall on your left, which takes you along the top of the Combe and then descends to some trees and crosses the Colly Brook via a footbridge. This is a lovely place to linger on a hot day - it is delightfully cool among the trees, with the brook tumbling over the rocks at your feet.

Go up the other side of the brook, and at the junction go straight on through the gate. You are now back on the path you took on the outward journey. Follow it back to the lane, past the cottages and down the hill. Just after you cross the stream turn right down the path which runs alongside it back to the road junction.

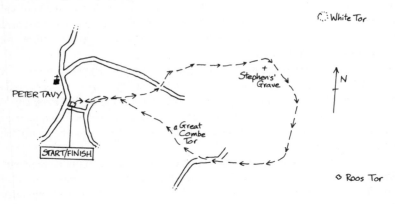

20. Lady Howard's Penance

OKEHAMPTON CASTLE

THE STORY

Poor Mary Howard is a much-maligned lady, who appears to have been condemned to an eternal penance for crimes she did not commit. Her story is a mixture of historical fact, mistaken identity and legend.

The historical fact is that she was the granddaughter of Sir John Fitz of Fitzford, Tavistock - the same Sir John who gave his name to Fice's Well (see Walk 5) - and that she was married four times. According to the story, she poisoned two of her husbands (and some versions say that she also murdered two of her children), and this is where the mistaken identity comes in. For there was also a Lady *Frances* Howard living at the same time, who really was accused of murder by poisoning, and was actually sent to the Tower of London for her crime. Lady *Mary*'s only offence seems to have been that she disinherited her children for reasons that are now unknown.

Now for the legend. Despite her innocence, the poor woman is said to have been condemned to travel each night from Fitzford House to Okehampton Castle and return with one blade of grass. Only when all the grass has been removed will her penance be over. She travels in the guise of an enormous black dog, which runs alongside a coach made from the bones of her murdered husbands, drawn by headless black horses and driven by a headless coachman. In some versions, she rides inside the coach. And if you chance to see the coach going by, you will notice that it passes in absolute silence - there is no sound of hooves or wheels or harness.

THE WALK

Start and finish: Sourton Church, up a track opposite the Highwayman Inn on the A386 Tavistock-Okehampton road

Parking: There is a limited amount of parking by the church.

Length: 17km (10½ miles)

Approximate time: 4½ - 5 hours

Degree of difficulty: C

Route summary: To follow the whole of Lady Howard's route would be too long - it is almost 30km (about 18 miles) from Tavistock to Okehampton. We therefore join it at Sourton for what is arguably the most interesting section. Our route follows the King Way, the ancient highway along the western edge of Dartmoor, to Okehampton Castle, and then returns via the moors. It takes in farm tracks, woodland ways, riverside paths and some of the wildest moorland on Dartmoor. The views are magnificent, and if you are prepared to undertake the stiff climb up Yes Tor you will be rewarded with a stunning 360 degree panorama.

The return part of this walk takes you across Okehampton Range. You should therefore check on firing times before setting out. If there is a red flag flying from Yes Tor when you come out of Okehampton Camp (see the detailed route description below), then there is no alternative but to retrace your outward route. If there is no flag flying, then it is quite safe to proceed.

Go up the track to the right of the church (signposted 'bridlepath'). You will see Sourton Tors straight ahead. Cross the bridge over a dismantled railway and go straight on up the track and through a gate, with a wall on either side. When the walls diverge, go straight on for a short distance until the broad path you are on crosses another one. Go left here, so that you are walking below Sourton Tors and roughly parallel to the stone wall over on your left. This is the King Way. There is an extensive view across to your left along here, stretching all the way to Bodmin Moor in Cornwall.

Soon you will see a strange, almost conical, rock ahead of you near the corner of a wall. Go left here, following the wall on your right to a gate in the far corner. Go through it (signposted 'bridlepath') onto a track between two walls. You can look across to the wild and barren open moor on your right and the more gentle patchwork of fields and hedges to your left.

At the end of the track, go through a gate into a field, and at the end of the field go right (signposted to Meldon Reservoir). This path takes you round the end of a wall and along the foot of South Down. Soon the great spoil tips of Meldon Quarry come into view through the trees ahead. You go through an opening in the line of trees in front of you onto a track, and Meldon Reservoir appears on your right. The track takes you downhill alongside a wall. Where a path goes off to the right, you go straight on (signposted to the car park). Go through a gate, across a road and through another gate. Keep straight on (signposted to Meldon Viaduct). The quarry is now clearly visible up ahead, and soon you will see the impressive iron viaduct half left.

There is a steep descent to a gap in a wall, leading into a small wood. Go through the wood, and as the trees open out turn right to cross a footbridge over

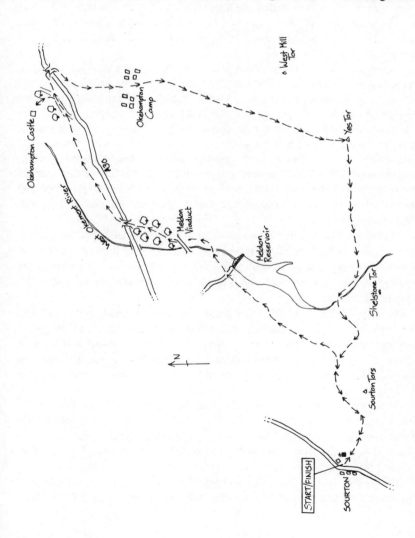

the West Okement River. Once across, turn immediately left. The viaduct towers over you as you make your way through the gorse to a gate and out onto a track and into some more woodland. The track joins a road and you go left to pass under the viaduct (signposted to the A30). A short distance beyond the viaduct, go right onto a path (signposted 'permitted bridlepath'). This path at first climbs away from the road and then runs roughly parallel to it through some dense, cool woodland, finally rejoining it just before the A30.

Turn right and follow the road round to the left as it crosses the A30. On the other side, go right (signposted to Okehampton), through a gate onto a track, which crosses three fields to a farm. Cross the farmyard to a gate (signposted 'path') and follow the fence round to the left to bypass the farm buildings and join another track.

When the track peters out, keep following the fence on your left until you come to a gate leading onto Okehampton Golf Course. The path leads straight across the golf course, and is clearly visible. You should keep strictly to it, and beware of golf balls as you go. As you make your way across, you will see Okehampton Castle half left. At the end of the golf course, you join a road. It crosses a cattle grid and enters a wood. Soon after it does so, you should go left onto a path (signposted to the castle and Okehampton). This is a lovely stretch, running down to the West Okement, and as you go, you will see the castle across the river through the trees. At the bottom, cross the river via a footbridge and then go left to a gate. At the road just beyond the gate, turn left and Okehampton Castle is on your left.

It is an interesting old ruin, which dates back to Norman times. Its heyday, however, was under the Courtenay family, who held it from the fourteenth to the sixteenth century. It is now an English Heritage property and for a modest fee you can explore it, accompanied by a free tape commentary. The view from the keep is particularly good.

When you leave the castle, turn right to retrace your steps along the road, and then right again just before the car park to go back to the river. Go through the gate and turn left alongside the river to the footbridge. Cross it and go straight on up into the woods (signposted to Meldon Viaduct and Tors Road), still retracing the route along which you came. At the fork in the paths, go left, back up to the road.

When you get to the road, instead of turning right, back to the golf course, go left (signposted to Tors Road). After about 50m, bear right off the road onto a path (signposted 'footpath Tors Road'). Go through the gate at the end onto a road and turn right. The road climbs steeply and curves left to cross a railway line and then right to cross the A30.

On the other side of the A30, turn immediately right down a small side road (signposted 'public footpath'). Just before the gate at the end, go left. The road becomes a track leading up to a house. Just before you get to the house, fork right onto another track and cross a stile. On the other side, bear left off the track (signposted to Okehampton Camp). The path climbs steeply in amongst some trees, and then emerges onto Okehampton Park. When you reach the top, there is a quite magnificent view across West and North Devon to the right and behind you, and Okehampton Camp appears ahead.

Cross to the camp gate and follow the road straight ahead. You may be stopped at the guard house and pointed in the right direction to cross the camp, but whether or not you are stopped, do not leave the road. This is a military complex, and only the marked route is a public right of way. At the top of the road, bear left, following the wooden 'path' sign, and at the T-junction turn right (signposted 'path' again). At the top, where the road goes to the right, bear left to a stile, again following the direction indicated by a wooden 'path' sign. Cross the field on the other side to another stile and cross that onto the open moor.

You will see two tors ahead of you: West Mill Tor in the foreground and Yes Tor behind it and slightly to the right. It is unlikely that you will have been allowed to get this far on firing days, but to be on the safe side, look at the summit of Yes Tor. If there is a flag flying from the flagpole there, then firing is taking place and you should not proceed. If there is no flag, then it is safe to go on.

It is Yes Tor you should be making for, initially along the tarred military track. When the track starts to curve round to the left of West Mill Tor, strike off to the right, across the open moor. There is no path, but the going is relatively easy, if a bit wet in places. Keep aiming for Yes Tor as you climb gently over the lower slopes of West Mill Tor. This is the 'real' Dartmoor - bare, wild and awesome.

There is an excellent outlook over to your right, but for a truly spectacular view, you should climb Yes Tor. It is not an easy climb, and you have to negotiate some fairly rocky ground, but when you get to the top you are rewarded with an incredible 360 degree panorama, with only High Willhays (the highest point on Dartmoor, just 2m higher than Yes Tor) slightly obscuring the view to the south. It looks as though the whole of Devon is laid out before you, and much of it is - certainly most of the northern, eastern and western parts of the county, as well as a large slice of eastern Cornwall and parts of Somerset.

If you are daunted by the prospect of the climb, however, you can follow the lower slopes of Yes Tor round to the right and rejoin the route to the right of it.

From Yes Tor, turn right, heading due west, towards the unmistakable outline of Sourton Tors in the middle distance. If you have contoured round the lower slopes, then you should also look out for Sourton Tors as you round Yes Tor. Aim initially for them. Then, as you come further round, Shelstone Tor will appear, lower down, slightly to the left of Sourton Tors and nearer to you. Adjust your line slightly and make for that. Since Sourton Tors and Shelstone Tor are the only outcrops to be seen to your right as you come round, they are easy landmarks to find.

As you go down into the valley of the West Okement River, the ground becomes rather rough and boggy, but it is still quite easy to negotiate. At the bottom you will find a track running alongside the river. Turn right onto it and towards the end you will find a footbridge over the river on your left. Cross it and curve round to the right of the ridge on your left, following the stream which flows into the West Okement. Do not cross the stream and follow the river, otherwise you will end up back at Meldon Reservoir.

Near the head of the stream, you will see a wall coming down on the other side. Find a convenient place to cross and follow the line of the wall. Where it bends to the right you will come across the conical rock you noticed on the outward journey. Turn left onto the broad, grassy path and soon you will find another wall running parallel to you on your right, with Sourton Tors over on your left. This is the path you went out on. When the wall goes off to the right, follow it round and follow the track through the gate and back to Sourton Church.